TRICURIOUS

Summersdale Publishers Ltd
46 West Street
Chichester
West Sussex
PO19 1RP
UK

www.summersdale.com

Printed and bound by CPI Group (UK) Ltd, Croydon, CR0 4YY

ISBN: 978-1-84953-714-8

Substantial discounts on bulk quantities of Summersdale books are available to corporations, professional associations and other organisations. For details contact Nicky Douglas by telephone: +44 (0) 1243 756902, fax: +44 (0) 1243 786300 or email: nicky@summersdale.com.

TRICURIOUS

Surviving the Deep End, Getting into Gear and Racing to Triathlon Success

Laura Fountain
and Katie King

summersdale

*For our nieces and nephews – seek out
adventures and good friends to join you*

Contents

Introduction

Laura

Two days after I failed to finish Ironman UK, I climbed on my bike and cycled 20 miles through the Lake District. Part way through my cycle, I stopped by Coniston Water, propped my bike up against a tree, and waded out into the lake for a swim. This wasn't training. There was no training plan urging me to do it and no longer a race on the horizon to prepare for. I was cycling and swimming because, over the past couple of years, swimming, cycling and running had become regular parts of my week. They weren't just training or a way to get fitter or stronger, they were things I did because I enjoyed doing them. They were automatic responses to the sun being out or me feeling a bit restless. They were a way to relax, to hang out with friends, or to have a few moments by myself. They'd made my life richer in more ways than I'd expected.

Signing up for a triathlon changed my life in many ways. I would urge you to sign up for one immediately and throw yourself fully into thoroughly enjoying the journey to get there. To love the feeling of the wind flying through your hair on the bike, the cool water against your skin, and the ground beneath your feet. Because race day is just one day, there are many days to enjoy on the road to your race and many more on the other side. If you hang up your goggles, lock your bike up in the shed and throw away your trainers as soon as you've met your goal, you've missed the point of the journey.

I've heard and read many people describe the satisfaction that they experienced on finishing a long-distance triathlon. While I would eventually finish an iron-distance swim, cycle and run, the moments along the way to get there were worth more than any medal. What follows is the story of how triathlon made me love swimming, cycling and running. It was a tall order given that I couldn't swim, barely ran and rarely cycled when I misguidedly signed up for my first event.

I met a lot of people along the way. None more significant than Katie King. She was the first real-life triathlete I knew. We met online through a shared interest in running marathons and drinking beer. Katie is without doubt the most modest person I know. It took a few years of knowing her until I found out that she's got a PhD from Oxford University in some very specific thing about the heart ('Well it's not the sort of thing that often comes up in conversation'). Or that she'd cycled from John O' Groats to Land's End for a bit of a laugh ('It was quite a while ago and I was a lot fitter then'). So, when she said to me after her own iron-distance triathlon, 'Yeah of course you can do it, it's fine,' I didn't know if this was another case of classic Katie modesty.

Because she's so modest, I'm going to tell you some of her athletic achievements. She rowed for Oxford in the Women's Boat Race (2nd crew). She won the 'Traditional' (un-wetsuited) category in the Henley Swim 5 km. And, possibly most impressive of them all, she once held in a fart for the entire duration of a marathon.

There are people that you'll meet at the start of races who will tell you, without prompting, every ailment they have, every training session they've missed and why they probably won't be 'in PB form' that day. Katie is not one of these people. She tells the story of how, 27 miles into the Connemara Ultra Marathon, a lady drew alongside her, wearing unfathomably tiny shorts, keen to talk about her sore calves, her sore back, and her blisters, and about how desperate she was for the race to end. 'And you?' the lady asked Katie. Unsure whether the polite response was one of mutual negativity, Katie simply offered, 'My knickers are chafing a bit.' Solemn silence fell and Katie looked bashfully at her shoes, wondering if she'd shared too much. The lull was broken as the other runner skipped ahead with, 'Well, I'm fine. I don't wear any anyway.' Katie vowed to learn from this and offer details of a different sore bit when asked again in future.

When Katie did an iron-distance triathlon for the first time I had no doubt she'd finish it. Not because it came easily to her (it didn't), or because she's a naturally gifted athlete (I know she won't mind me saying, she's not), but because she doesn't give up, she doesn't make excuses and she doesn't complain.

If you want to do something amazing, surround yourself with amazing people. Whether it's running a marathon, cycling 100 miles, or swimming the Channel – if you start hanging round with people who think that your dreams sound like a great way to spend your weekends, rather than those who question why you'd want to do such a thing, you'll find those dreams become a reality a lot sooner.

I've met some pretty amazing women over the past few years. Women who enjoy being active and doing stuff. Women for whom the idea of running a marathon is one to be met with excitement and encouragement. Whose only response to the question, 'Fancy going for a bike ride?' is 'Yeah, how far?'

I didn't know anyone else who ran when I started running. But I found them through running clubs, Twitter and the blogs I read. If you don't know anyone who does the stuff you want to do – people who climb mountains, run or cycle a long way – go find some. Go join a running or triathlon club, visit a parkrun, or find them online. Above all, seek out people with the attitude to life that you want for yourself. Surround yourself with people who don't care what their bum looks like in cycling shorts and you'll start to care less about your own. Surround yourself with positive people and you'll become more positive yourself. Surround yourself with people who say 'Yes!' to adventures, and you'll find yourself going on more of them.

If you want to do a triathlon, first find yourself a friend like Katie; someone who loves the sport, who encourages you to get stuck into it, and who will patiently answer all your questions. Katie has distilled her triathlon experience into this book. Hopefully, it will answer all the questions you might have about the sport and encourage you to give it a go.

Katie

Laura did ask a lot of questions. Perhaps the most intriguing one of all was, 'Do you want to write a book with me about triathlon?'

I'm not a coach. I'm not an elite. I am a bit squidgy around the edges. But, as Laura explains, if people who think your goals are a good idea surround you, your dreams become a reality much sooner; I'm just lucky that I have always been surrounded by those people.

I grew up with two very sporty older brothers and two parents who were, and still are, completely devoted to supporting our interests. My eldest brother was on the British triathlon junior squad for four years; he finally achieved his aim to qualify for the World Championships in his final year as a junior in 1993. Much to his disappointment, the championships that year were to be held in Manchester; not that there's anything wrong with Manchester, but the 1991 and 1992 championships had been held in Australia and Canada, respectively. Still, it did mean that we all got to go along and cheer. Every cloud, and all that.

Until then, I'd had a curious interest in triathlon. Inspired by my brothers, my mum took it up after learning to swim in her 40s and it soon became a whole family affair, with my dad doing a sterling job transporting us around the country in the very early hours of most Sunday mornings. I joined in with the swim sessions with our local triathlon club, got in the way at social events, and cheered from the sidelines at races while wanting, as all good little sisters do, to get involved with anything my brothers were up to.

In Manchester, there was a kids' triathlon being held on the same weekend as my brother's event, and so my dad signed me up to my first race, aged 13. While the details are a bit hazy, I mostly remember that the bike course was off-road, so I rode my Raleigh Monterey (a pink bike that I'd ridden into many a ditch in the woods previously) and I remember a woman saying, 'Oh bless her!' and trying to push the back of my saddle as I went up a hill. I was quite cross about this. So when my dad leapt out with the camcorder, videoing the whole thing, I think I might have muttered one of my very first swear words under my breath. Sorry, Dad. Before fitness apps were available for your phone, there were scrapbooks, and recently my mum dug out the results and photographs from my race more than 20 years ago: I was fifth out of seven and, judging by the look on my face, the photo appears to have been taken shortly after that lady tried to push me. Incidentally, the video of that race has mysteriously never been aired.

With hindsight, taking part in my first triathlon aged 13 was pretty bad timing for me. Firstly, this was the early 1990s when triathletes ran around in their swimming costumes, which was ironic really when you consider how fashionable the cycling short was around that time, regardless of whether you owned a bike. Entering the awkward teenage years, I had opted to save my dignity by throwing a massive black T-shirt and pair of baggy Bermuda shorts over my swimming costume, which no doubt cost me those valuable seconds in wind-resistance and transition time. Perhaps if I was less shy, I could have been fourth! There was, however, a more pressing issue that kept me from taking part in another triathlon.

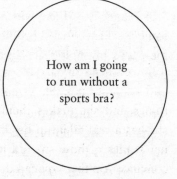

Things that worry many people before doing their first triathlon

Things that worried me about doing another triathlon

I swam competitively with a club until I was 14 and then started rowing: a sport that kept me busy for the next few years, and offered a great distraction from things like essays and revision once I got to university. I rode my bike across Oxford to get to training, and running was a way to keep fit when the river was in flood so, after graduating, when I realised that I was struggling to fit rowing in around more 'normal' working hours, I looked for other sporting challenges: running marathons and road cycling both caught my attention. It was two good friends, who I met through cycling in my 20s, who finally convinced me to do another triathlon. Helen had raced two Ironman events in Canada. She was officially the toughest person I knew but one piece of her advice really stuck with me: enjoy your first event and then you will want to do another. Rachel was another former GB junior triathlete with lots of race experience. She had retired from triathlons and was taking some scalps in road cycling, but she helped me through my first two sprint triathlons, answering my questions, normally with some wonderful no-nonsense responses. Crucially, they both agreed on one matter that sealed the deal for me: you can wear a sports bra under your kit.

I didn't know Laura before she became a runner, but I've followed her story from sofa to marathon, through her blog and her first book. She is one of life's do-ers: she gets on with things and she makes them happen. Beyond that, however, she has a real talent in her honest and hilarious ability to tell her stories of how she did it; stories that sweep you up and convince you that you can do it too. Whether she writes about training, races, success or disappointment, she draws on her experiences to encourage others, to teach them to run, and to love it. Our mutual friend, Liz, describes how Laura, upon her return from hospital to have a breast lump removed under general anaesthetic, sent her a text to inform her that she had gone out on her scheduled 18 mile training run, wearing three sports bras and dosed up on painkillers. If any other friend had sent the same message, she would have worried, but we understood why Laura needed to run that day. Perhaps even more impressive was the world's fastest ever turnaround from a hangover the morning after the Frankfurt marathon, just in time to fly home in gale force winds. She's terrified of flying but this was just another case of Laura doing what she needed to do. So when Laura told me she fancied doing a triathlon, there was only one way this was going to go.

When you take up something new, there's often a balance between asking questions and finding things out for yourself. As Laura took up triathlon, she asked plenty. The practical questions were easy to answer but she asked plenty of bigger ones too: ones that dared us both to take risks. In doing so, she's also answered many of my questions. As Laura tells the story of her transformation from a non-swimmer, who was once scared of water, to a triathlete, I hope we can answer a few of yours too.

KATIE

From midday sun to Midnight Man: Going the extra mile

Shivering in the pouring rain, with my bike propped against a traffic cone, and snot dripping from my nose, I attempted to fix another puncture in the dark. I'd covered nearly 80 miles on my bike by then and was growing acutely aware of how few people there were left behind me on the course. When things go wrong in a race, there are two real choices: 1) Worry: 'What if I'm last? Can I really do this? Would it really matter if I packed up and went home?' or, 2) Just get on with it. As long as I could get moving again, there was still every chance I could finish. I'd covered far further than 80 miles on my bike in training to get to this point.

• • •

My friend, Acer, who I knew from rowing at university, took on Ironman Nice on the hottest day of 2009. One third of the way into the bike course, and halfway up the biggest climb of the day, his chain snapped. With the nearest race mechanic 10 km away at the top of the next pass, the marshals told him to give up. Instead, he jogged until someone loaned him a tool to rejoin the chain and then completed the remaining 100 km on a fraction of the gears he started with. All this before running a marathon. He took a photograph of himself at the start of the day and posted it in his Facebook album from the event; I keep it by my computer at work and cherish the caption as much as the picture itself:

> 'Day 3: Happy! (Whatever may be in store for me today, at least I'm not stuck behind a desk in an air-conditioned office under artificial light in front of a computer screen...)'

When the alarm went off at 5.15 on a sticky Sunday morning in August 2012, it wasn't as much to wake me up, as to signal that it was time to stop trying to get any sleep at all. With France in the grips of a European heatwave, our budget hotel room near the race start would have made the innards of a Thermos flask look pretty draughty in comparison. I peeled myself from the sheets and forced down some breakfast before my boyfriend drove me to the start area.

I wandered down towards transition, where my trusty bike had been stowed overnight, and noticed that The Eagles' 'Hotel California' was playing out through the darkness. It seemed fitting that such a relentlessly long song was being played ahead of what should be the longest race of my life. Completing an iron-distance triathlon, with a 3.8 km swim, 180 km bike and a 42 km run, had been an ambition long before any actual committed effort to run more than a half marathon began a few years earlier. On our bike rides to the river as students, Acer and I established our mutual interest in cycling. We laughed at the noises our student bikes made as we rode out to the river for training, both contraptions we'd owned since our early teens. Since graduating, we coveted and congratulated each other on the upgrades over the years; we swapped stories of accidents, adventures and ambitions on two wheels; and we shared an aspiration to complete an ironman. Acer had got around to his goal much sooner than me but, after eight months of training, and a long drive from Oxford to central France, I was going to have a go at achieving this at a race called Challenge Vichy.

The temperature inside our car had risen steadily as we drove through France the week before, until we finally stepped out into scorching sunshine in the dusty car park in Vichy. Sweat dripped uncomfortably down my back as I signed up for my number and tried to interpret some of the complicated French race instructions. *It's just a bit sunny, right? I can do this.* I bought a white running cap at the expo and promised myself I'd keep drinking water. A Friday morning swim in the lake and a short cycle up the only tangible climb on the course both calmed and cooled the nerves. The water temperature had been recorded that morning at 24°C, the maximum temperature allowed before wetsuits are no longer permitted. A decision would be made about whether we could wear them on the morning of the race, and relayed to competitors then.

Temperatures reached the high 30s on Saturday and, with no breeze, just moving about in the sunshine was taking some considerable effort, and creating some impressive perspiration. 'This is France in August,' said my boyfriend, trying to reassure me that it was entirely my decision to sign up for this.

I took my bike to the transition area, where a concerned looking marshal was handing out pieces of paper to competitors. On them were written the organiser's plans for tomorrow's conditions. Race day was expected to reach more than 40°C so we were being briefed that we may be taken off the course and checked over at any time by the medical staff. Essentially, they could withdraw us from the race at any time if they thought we were in danger. They also reserved the right to stop the race for everyone at any point. We were only to start the race if we were, 'In perfects conditions [sic] and in full possession of your faculties'.

So, in the darkness on Sunday morning, grateful for some relative cool before the sun came up, I sipped water nervously, questioning my conditions and faculties, and waited for the final announcement about wetsuits. An English-speaking volunteer spoke up on the PA system, 'Ladies and gentlemen. As you are aware, we are in a Grade 2 heatwave. As such the organisers of Challenge Vichy have decided to cut the distance to a half ironman.'

I stood still, letting the news sink in, pulling the same face I'd make if I'd just dropped a big piece of chocolate cake on the floor, buttercream icing face down. At first, nerves were replaced by disappointment, frustration and a slight urge to have a bit of a cry; then, a resolution to pick up the cake from the floor (the 5-second rule applies in analogies too) and bloody well enjoy it anyway, reassured by the knowledge that this bit of cake was less likely to leave me in hospital on a drip.

To sum up the rest of the day, it was like turning up your central heating, switching the oven on, and jogging around the house in a thick coat until it feels like the room has reached 43°C. Then keeping at it for another 8 hours. Nevertheless, a big highlight for me was the swim start: I had heard a lot about mass starts at big races so I'm glad I got to experience what it's like to race with several hundred people in the water at the same time. Women were marked out by our pink swimming hats and the race video I watched afterwards confirmed my suspicion of how few of us there were competing in the male-dominated field. The water can take on a strange consistency with all that testosterone in it and, unless you're out at the front, you're unlikely to find any space of your own to swim in. Flailing arms and legs were everywhere, but it takes more than a few aggressive boys to scare me in the water and the experience was little short of awesome. The run along the banks of the river was unforgiving in the heat of the early afternoon but we were well looked-after with regular water stations and showers to run through. I spent the final 10 km chatting to a man from Paris who had been forced to pull out of an iron-distance race the year before with dehydration; he was philosophical about this year's event but clearly disappointed. I finished, finding my boyfriend in a worse state than me; him having spent the best part of the day stood cheering in the ruthless heat, without the benefit of those frequent water stops.

Sipping a cold beer with half an ironman completed, it was tempting to feel frustrated with the decision made and disappointed with a goal not realised, not to mention the 300 euro entry fee for only half a race. I had a medal that said I was iron and a conscience that knew I wasn't. Shortly after the event, the organisers published details of the decision process leading up to the race and, after reading this, I was certain they had made the right decision to shorten it. Four volunteers alone had collapsed the afternoon before, helping to set up the event. The decision to shorten the race, rather than to stop it halfway, allowed competitors the opportunity to cross a finishing line; however disappointing, this was a more satisfying experience than a forced DNF (the abbreviation on results that states you 'Did not finish') and our safety was priority throughout. The event was superbly organised, which you'd be right to expect from such a huge entry fee, but this and the commitment and enthusiasm of the volunteers, made it a very enjoyable race.

I deliberated over entering another event for some time. Challenge Vichy offered an entry to the event again in 2013 but I wasn't keen to repeat the same experience; the UK version of the Challenge event also offered a few pounds off their entry fee to race the following month but I couldn't justify another £300 on another race entry in the same year. Training for Vichy had taken months: laps and laps of my local watersports lake, trying to up my swim mileage; turning up to a friend's hen night 4 hours late in cycle kit; long runs in the evening after an even longer day at work. It was an enjoyable and positive experience but one that took dedication and compromise, and the decision to enter another race was something I couldn't take lightly.

I found out Acer was ill while I was training for Vichy. The day I heard the news, I rode my bike. I rode my bike and I thought of him. I rode my bike and I worried about him. I rode my bike and I questioned why he hadn't told us. I rode my bike and I got angry. I rode my bike until I came to the conclusion that he'd tell us directly if things were that bad. I told myself that everything would be OK; he would tell us if it wasn't. That conversation never happened and Acer passed away early in 2013. Sometimes these decisions are made for us. I remembered the conversations we used to have as we rode our bikes to the river to go training, and our mutual ambition to complete an iron-distance triathlon. I remembered how he had completed his and I decided I would enter another as my own quiet tribute to him.

Having experienced the hullabaloo of a large, branded European race, I looked around and found details of a small, British event, known as the Midnight Man. Taking place through the night in Dartford in July 2013, it was unlikely to suffer the consequences of a heatwave, and its low key nature meant that the entry fee was a mere fraction of the cost of the bigger races. No driving across Europe req uired, nor budget hotel rooms near the race venue; the 6 p.m. kick-off just required a trip around the M25 that afternoon and no need to book a bed for the night.

Nearly twelve months later, the start of this event couldn't have been more different to that early morning in France. A small marquee and finishing gantry marked the event HQ, with a burger van parked up under a mobile floodlight to nourish the supporters and marshals through the night; apparently, in the small hours of the following morning, some local revellers were so overjoyed to find the van in an otherwise desolate estate, they made a vocal plea to have a triathlon there every weekend. Heavy rain was forecast for the evening and the organiser warned that, in the event of lightning, the lake may have to be evacuated during the swim; a very different type of weather warning to that written on the piece of paper in Vichy. Still, one that made me question my faculties once again. I was utterly terrified: terrified that I was unprepared; terrified that I was out of my depth; terrified that my body wouldn't cope and that I wouldn't finish. I made a quiet promise to Acer that I'd do my best and remember him throughout: how he faced his fears; how he conquered difficulties; how he remained grateful that he wasn't stuck behind a desk in an air-conditioned office under artificial light in front of a computer screen. At 6.15 on the Saturday evening, I started my next attempt at an iron-distance race in the full knowledge that I would still be racing while others slept, and when they woke again on Sunday morning.

Even with a half iron-distance event running alongside in the swim start, there was plenty of space to swim and the atmosphere seemed somehow more convivial than the thrashing and kicking in France a year earlier; that said, the sky grew progressively darker as the laps ticked by and the rain started to flick down on the lake during my last 800 m. After a discreet change out of my wetsuit into some bike shorts with a chamois that would stand the test of 180 km, I was out of transition and starting the 20-lap bike course with thunder rolling overhead. Consisting of an H-shaped loop, each lap had four out and back sections along some of Dartford's finest pieces of dual carriageway. Flat throughout, the only real climb was a hop onto the timing mat on each lap; however, some nifty cornering was needed to stay upright on the hairpin turns in the rapidly deteriorating conditions. A central roundabout in the first half of the lap provided the perfect spot for a loyal team of supporters – requiring Laura, and our very patient boyfriends, to stand in the rain, shouting encouragement as competitors rode past in three different directions; in fact, such was their eagerness to cheer all competitors that Laura, the most enthusiastic of all, seemed to be facing the wrong way every time I rode through. She later told me she was eating chips at the time, and that she had to placate some angry motorists, furious on their return from holiday that this particular piece of dual carriageway was closed to any traffic other than the foolish minority on bikes. All races need a supporter like Laura.

Continuous rain throughout the night meant plenty of debris was washed down the road and punctures became inevitable for almost all competitors; for every person I passed on the side of the road, I felt a funny mix of sympathy for them, guilt for not helping, and relief that it wasn't me. The relief was short-lived when I felt the classic rumbling of a wheel rim on tarmac almost immediately after crossing the halfway point. Changing an inner tube with cold wet hands at midnight was not exactly my idea of a fun Saturday night but was necessary in order to keep moving forwards. My repair work didn't last long enough and another puncture soon followed a couple of laps later; this time, away from the floodlit finish area, and next to that soggy roundabout instead, overlooked by two security guards with marshalling honours, wondering why on earth I'd put myself through this. When things go wrong in a race, there are two real choices: 1) Worry, or 2) Just get on with it.

With three laps to go, the most cheerful man you'd ever expect to meet on a bike in the middle of a thunderstorm during the small hours of a Sunday morning cycled alongside me and started chatting. He hadn't suffered any punctures but he had fallen off his bike earlier in the race; ever the optimist, he had climbed back on and continued riding. He rode with me for a while, telling me not to worry about the lightning – apparently, it would strike the QE2 Bridge before it hit us. I thanked him for his positive thoughts but decided not to tell him that it rained so hard that I'd managed to do a wee while still riding my bike (taking care to remove the bottle from its holder on the bike frame beneath me first) just moments before.

I don't think I've ever been so relieved to start running a marathon, let alone one that would start at 3.30 a.m. and take in eight laps on an industrial estate. I professed this fact to every runner I saw for the next half an hour, to which one replied, 'You're on your first lap, aren't you? Just wait.'

On lap two, I think I found out what he meant when I fell asleep momentarily while running; only the thud of the next footfall woke me up. I contemplated lying down for 10 minutes, just to satisfy the desperate urge to nod off, but thought it safer to keep fighting it; when the sun started to rise shortly before 5 a.m., it was somehow easier to convince myself that sleep wasn't necessary just yet. I smiled at and chatted to any other runners who'd listen; this included a competitor who, after he finished, kindly drove around the run course to find me before he left, to tell me to enjoy the rest of my morning. I ran every step, even when my boyfriend was able to walk faster than me while carrying a rucksack and a deckchair; partly out of pride and a determination that this should be a run, not a walk, but also a sense of urgency as I saw more and more people finish on every lap. I ran past the finishing line seven times before I was actually allowed to finish, each time growing more and more aware that I must be one of the last remaining competitors on the course. At 10 a.m., I finished my first iron-distance triathlon smiling and well over an hour before the 17-hour race cut-off.

When I decided to enter such a small race, a friend warned against it, saying, 'There's a very high chance of coming last, Katie.' Sixty-five people were listed on the start list on the Saturday evening but, as I have learned, plenty of things can go wrong in a race and only 29 finished. I was 29th. I learned more about myself, my patience, resilience, and determination, by coming last in that race than in any other sporting event where I've placed midfield, top ten, or even won. For all the flashy merchandise and enormous crowds at the famous, big-branded events, you'll rarely receive a handshake on the finish from a kinder, more dedicated race organiser in the business than at the Midnight Man, let alone an email later that week congratulating you on becoming, in his words, a 'true ironlady'. Finishing last in a race is not something that should put anyone off. If it's the difference between doing something and not, I would rather take last any day, especially when there's a promise to a friend that must be kept.

LAURA

The promise of a triathlon: How it all began

One Saturday morning in July, I stood by the side of the Serpentine Lido in Hyde Park putting on my wetsuit. It was a drizzly morning and I was in no rush to get into the water which, on that day, smelt like potato peelings. A man on the bench next to me struggling with his own wetsuit struck up conversation.

'Are you training for something?' he asked (he had a French accent if you'd like to imagine it).

'Yes, I've got a triathlon in two weeks. How about you?'

'I have a sprint triathlon in Belgium.' (Come to think of it, maybe it was a Belgian accent).

We chatted about triathlons for a bit. I told him I'd done one earlier in the summer in the very lake we were about to swim in. He said he wanted to do that one as he only lives round the corner. And then, as he was heading off to get into the water, he said: 'Good luck with your race. Which one is it?'

'It's Ironman UK, in Bolton.'

He turned back towards me, looked me up and down, raised his eyebrows, turned down the sides of his mouth and then said 'Good luck' again.

I wasn't offended by the look. It wasn't one that said 'I don't believe you' or 'No chance *mon amie*'. It was a look that was slightly surprised and intrigued. He obviously had a preconceived idea of what an ironman looks like and it didn't look anything like me. I'm 5 ft 5 in., I'm not at all muscly, and I'm a woman; the word 'ironman' doesn't conjure up that image. Until fairly recently, I had no idea what an ironman looked like either, but I've met quite a few along the way.

Two years earlier, I'd got off the Tube at Canary Wharf station and there she was – in trainers, capri leggings and a T-shirt, she looked like any other after-work runner, yet she was anything but. First British winner of the Ironman World Championship, a title she held four times, and undefeated in 13 Ironman races, Chrissie Wellington is no ordinary person. She was happily chatting away to a fan by the ticket gates and posed with him for a picture with her trademark grin. I was heading to a running shop where Chrissie was giving a talk and I walked through the station behind her.

It was difficult to judge what, as someone who could barely swim a few lengths of the pool and cycled once every couple of weeks, I would be able to take home from the advice given by an athlete who is the best in the world at their sport. But Chrissie chatted with the room full of keen amateur level athletes, passing her enthusiasm for the sport on to them.

This meeting with Chrissie wasn't what first planted the idea of doing a triathlon in my head. A few years earlier I'd signed up for a sprint distance women-only triathlon. I'd been persuaded by some clever marketing copy or an article in a magazine that entering a triathlon was just the thing I needed to kickstart a new healthier lifestyle. The plan was that this triathlon would make me finally commit to getting off my bum and doing some exercise. This was 2008 and race entry wasn't always as advanced, nor the organisers as tech savvy, as they are today. I sent off my entry form through the post with a cheque (remember cheques?). Somehow, maybe divine intervention to stop me drowning, my envelope had come apart in the mail and my cheque was destroyed. The organisers told me to send it again – I didn't. I'd remembered that, while I could survive in the local pool for a few metres, I couldn't really swim and I hadn't run since school; even then, it wasn't for any significant distance or with any grace. The only part of the triathlon I would have been able to complete would have been the bike. I'd need significantly longer to prepare for the race than I'd originally thought.

Instead of sending off my entry form, I joined a gym. It seemed the safer option. The chances of me drowning, for a start, were much lower because it didn't have a pool.

I turned up to my gym induction wearing a pair of trainers that were two sizes too small and a T-shirt with the words 'Fight for your right to party' on the front. The first time I went on a treadmill I could barely run for two minutes before I had to stop, but gradually, as I stuck with it, I started to progress and after six months I did a 10 km race. As I got better at running, and found I quite liked it, I forgot about triathlon. I quit the gym after a year but carried on running and, two years after that first shaky start on the treadmill, I ran my first marathon. It took five more marathons until I finally got round to filling in another entry form for a sprint distance triathlon. That's how I found myself on a rainy weekday evening sitting in a room full of people eager to hear what Chrissie Wellington had to say.

Chrissie was only the third triathlete I'd ever met. The first was Katie, whose laid-back approach and enthusiasm for the sport made it sound more like a daytrip to the seaside than an athletic endeavour. When I first voiced my plan to do a triathlon to Katie, she was enthusiastic. I suspect there are two reasons for this. It's like anything you feel passionate about – when you've heard an album that you really like, you want all your friends to listen to it too or if you're really engrossed in a TV series, you tell all your colleagues to watch it so you can discuss it in detail the next morning at work; it's pretty much the same thing with runners or triathletes.

The other reason is that there aren't many women doing triathlons. Of the 15,605 members of the British Triathlon Federation in 2013, just 4,155 were women. In the past couple of years, more women-only triathlon events have been popping up to try to encourage more female participants into the sport. Standing on the pontoon of a triathlon start in Hyde Park in June 2014, Katie and I looked round and tried to count the number of women in our wave. It's not always that easy to identify gender once you've been squished into a wetsuit and have put your swim hat and goggles on, but we were probably less than a quarter of the starters. I don't want to hypothesise as to why fewer women than men are signing up for triathlons, but I'd like to change that. And that started in a very small way by signing up for one myself.

I met Billy while I was training for my second marathon. Billy was the owner of the hotel I was staying at on holiday with my family in Greece and the second ironman that I met. We talked about training, he asked me about marathons and told me about triathlon. Billy was training for his first iron-distance triathlon when I met him and has since done many more. When he explained the distances involved in his race it made me feel sick at the thought of up to 17 hours of swimming, cycling and running. It seemed impossible. But then, on a rainy evening in London, I met Chrissie Wellington. As she shared the story of how she got started in triathlon and eventually went on to be the best in the world at the iron-distance, the overwhelming message was that we're all capable of much more than we think is possible. She urged the room of people to believe in themselves and push their boundaries. If you've ever seen the film *Cocoon* where the old people go swimming with the alien pods and come out of the water revitalised and full of life, that's what it's like meeting Chrissie Wellington. Her enthusiasm and belief is contagious. I started to believe that I could do a triathlon. And that's possibly why this very average marathon runner, who hadn't even done a sprint triathlon, promised her she'd do an ironman.

I could have said 'triathlon'. A triathlon of any length would still have been a big and worthwhile goal for me. A few years earlier, when I'd stepped into that basement gym for the first time, I'd been unable to run 400 metres without stopping but now I was running marathons. It had changed my perception of what was and wasn't possible for me and so, although I struggled with more than a few very splashy, face-out-the-water lengths of the local swimming pool, I reasoned that I might be able to get better at swimming. And then maybe, I'd be able to do an ironman. If nothing else I was going to give it my best shot and see what happened.

Chrissie wrote an inscription in the front of my copy of her book that reads, 'Laura. Never give up... You promised me!' When you make promises like that to the four-time Ironman World Champion, you kind of have to keep them.

KATIE

Going the distance:
How long is a triathlon?

I rarely call myself a triathlete: I'm just a person who loves the three sports, and once in a while, gets to do them all on the same day. You can be a runner without entering races, you can do the same as a cyclist or a swimmer. Therein lies the difference in triathlon: you are only ever a triathlete on race day. This is something that causes a little distrust from disciples of the pure sports. I guess it's a question of semantics, an issue within which we shall refrain from engaging in much deeper discussions here, but it means that the logical place to start seems to be with the event itself: a triathlon.

If you're not already familiar with it, triathlon is a multi-sport event where competitors participate in three consecutive endurance events: swimming, cycling and running. Races may take a variety of forms, but a standard order is normally adopted and events tend to vary, instead, by distance. The three parts can be compared to going out for a nice curry. The swim is like a pint of lager with a splashy start, a lot of bubbles, and it requires a bit of perseverance. The cycle, like poppadoms, can be considered the more technical of the three disciplines, requiring presence of mind and some skill to keep the mango chutney from spilling on the floor. The main course, or run, can become a bit of a slog if you have bitten off more than you can chew earlier in the event; however, a focused mind and some gritty determination will see you through to the end, where you can finally lie down and look back with satisfaction. It's a race against the clock for most, with the timer starting as you begin your swim and stopping as you finish the run; and this is where the analogy breaks down, if you want to avoid indigestion. There are a number of set distances for triathlons but each event can vary slightly depending on the organisers, the course and other constraints.

Supersprint distance

Ideal as an introduction to the event, the Supersprint distance is generally around a 400 m swim, 10 km cycle, and a 2.5 km run. Many race organisers offer a shorter novice distance to encourage people to 'Try a Tri'.

Sprint distance

The sprint distance is where a lot of people start and there is plenty to choose from. 'Sprint' is a curious way to describe this endurance event: Rebecca Adlington would not call a 750 m swim a sprint, Chris Hoy would laugh at being asked to sprint over 20 km and Mo Farah's 5 km pace might be a sprint for some but most of us could only keep that up if being chased by a tiger, let alone after a swim and a bike ride. Regardless of the misnomer, this is a great distance to start off with and many experienced triathletes continue to race competitively over this distance.

'Olympic' distance/standard distance

Triathlon has been an Olympic sport since Sydney 2000 and involves a standard 1,500 m swim, 40 km cycle, 10 km run. Despite its name, the 'Olympic' or standard distance event is popular with amateur athletes and a good challenge to work towards. When watching the Brownlee brothers in the Olympics, or any other elite field, you'll see one big difference to your own race: the elites have different rules on the bike leg and can work together in a pack, which can offer a tactical advantage and some rest when tucked in behind another competitor; this essentially means the result can come down to the 10 km run. Even though a standard distance event covers the same length course, we mere mortals work by a different set of rules in our races and the cycle will have a strict no-drafting rule, which means the whole event remains a race against the clock; the same is true in races of other distances too (see Hard and fast).

Half iron-distance/middle distance/'70.3'

This is exactly what the name suggests: it's half the distance of an iron-distance triathlon (see next page). Made up of a 1.9 km swim, 90 km cycle and a half marathon (21.1 km) run (or 70.3 miles in total, as in the branded 'Ironman 70.3' event name), this is a distance to be respected and will take a few hours out of your Sunday. The problem with this is that its moniker suggests it's 'only' half of something, which is a red rag to someone like me who sees that there's another half left that needs tackling. Races in this ballpark are also known as 'middle distance', which does little more to satisfy the curiosity of someone keen to find out where the limits lie. We suggested renaming it an 'ironboy' but it hasn't made much impact in the triathlon world so far.

Iron-distance/long-distance

The iron-distance triathlon is becoming a very popular distance and many people enter triathlon with this as their ultimate aim. It's amazing that this very specific distance (3.8 km swim, 180 km cycle, 42.2 km run) has so many people under its spell when you consider that its origin lies with a fairly random combination of three pre-existing endurance events on the island of Oahu in Hawaii. In a challenge to find out whether swimmers, cyclists or runners made the toughest endurance athletes, an event was organised where competitors would race over the 3.8 km Waikiki Roughwater Swim, 180 km of the Around-Oahu Bike Race and the 42.2 km Honolulu Marathon course on one day in February 1978. Known as 'Ironman', the race distance has become more and more popular since then. The official 'Ironman' moniker belongs to the World Triathlon Corporation (WTC), which stages the World Ironman Championships each year in Hawaii, as well as other events around the world. The term 'ironman', with a little 'i', is often used unofficially to describe a long-distance or iron-distance event of the same length. *Iron Man*, on the other hand, is a film starring Robert Downey Jr. The big branded events are expensive to enter but happen all over the world, and, for several hundred pounds in entry fees, plus travel and accommodation costs, competitors are guaranteed big crowds, a great atmosphere and some flashy merchandising. I think I might also want some small swimming baths named after me for that kind of money, so luckily there are more and more race organisers putting on lower key long-distance events with a reduced price tag.

Multiple iron-distance events

That's right. One ironman is simply not enough for some people. There are a few specialist events that multiply the iron-distance event into a gruelling ultra-triathlon option. These triathlons are either run as a continuous event with multiplied distances, or multiple iron-distance events one day after another. The 'Triple Deca Ironman' is an example of the latter, held in Italy in 2013, and consisting of 30 consecutive iron-distance triathlons on 30 consecutive days. You would be forgiven for thinking these races are solely the territory of a fearsome few who sleep with one eye open and eat nettles for breakfast, but I once met a terribly nice man, called Paul Parrish, who took on the double (7.6 km swim, 360 km cycle, 84 km run) when he felt he couldn't ask his friends for sponsorship for 'another ironman'. A year later he tackled the triple (11.4 km swim, 540 km cycle, 126 km run) when he wanted to go back again with his collection tin. Needless to say, the charity in question meant an awful lot to him. He juggled work and family life around preparing for each event and viewed the undertaking in its most simple terms, 'Whichever way you look at it, it's going to be a long day'.

As it was, the triple spanned nearly three entire days. What do you think about for that long? In Paul's words, 'I thought about life, about sandwiches, I even spent some time naming all the animals that I thought could be kept in a zoo without being upset by captivity. Most of them were quite small.' Not enough for you? In September 2014, at 49 years old, Paul also became the oldest solo challenger to complete the 'Arch to Arc' triathlon: a 140 km run from London's Marble Arch to Dover, a swim across the English Channel, and a 290 km cycle from Calais to the Arc de Triomphe in Paris.

Give us an inch and we'll take a kilometre

A pint might represent the triathlon swim in that earlier curry analogy but you can expect to see both imperial and metric units in race distances. Swim distances are often given in metres but the run and cycle might be in miles or kilometres. You're going to become bilingual when it comes to race distances because triathletes often switch between them so, to get you started, the run and cycle distances in this table are given in both.

Event	Swim	Bike	Run
Supersprint	400 m	10 km 6.2 miles	2.5 km 1.5 miles
Sprint	750 m	20 km 12.4 miles	5 km 3.1 miles
Olympic/ standard distance	1,500 m	40 km 24.9 miles	10 km 6.2 miles

Half-iron/ middle-distance	1,900 m	90 km 56 miles	21.1 km (half marathon) 13.1 miles
Iron-distance/ long-distance	3,800 m	180 km 112 miles	42.2 km (marathon) 26.2 miles
Ultra-distance (distances vary)	>3,800 m	>180 km >112 miles	>42.2 km >26.2 miles

Deciding on the distance you want to tackle will depend on your current fitness and a realistic view of where you want to get to between now and the time of your first event. Contacting your local club is a good idea for some advice and, while this can be an intimidating thought at first, there will be plenty of friendly people and coaches who were once in the same position as you, keen to help you on your way. The British Triathlon Federation website (www.britishtriathlon.org) can help you to locate a local club; it also has an event search, where you can enter a region and a distance and start looking for an event.

Your swimming confidence might well dictate the kind of event you want to start with: confident swimmers will enjoy the turmoil of an open-water swim but if you're more flail than fish then you may wish to start out with a pool swim. If you just want to dip your toe in before taking on the trinity, there are various combinations of just two of the disciplines: aquathlons

43

are a swim followed by a run and negate the need for a bike; duathlons, triathlon's drier cousins, cut out the swim with a run-cycle-run format; and the aquabike seems to be a relatively new permutation cropping up where competitors swim and cycle, often alongside a triathlon running on the same course. At the time of writing this, entering 'aquabike' into an Internet search returned a jet-skiing competition and a pool fitness fad involving twenty exercise bikes plopped in at the shallow end of the public baths; of course, either of these options might now appeal to you more than a triathlon and, if this the case, I wish you luck in all your future endeavours.

One further thing you might want to consider is how much money you'd like to spend. Entering the world of triathlon, you are embarking on a sporting journey that can cost rather more than you expected; however, selecting a race needn't require you to sell an organ. Generally speaking, the smaller club-run events are a less expensive option; they may not draw the big crowds but they are run by people who know the sport well and who put the competitors before profits. My local club, Oxford Tri, organises a sprint distance event that costs about £30. The larger, more commercial events might be more your style, and can offer some stunning locations and the possibility of closed roads for the cycle and run; however, you can expect to pay a lot more for these (Blenheim Triathlon costs more than £80 for a sprint distance race). Deciding on your race is a bit like buying your first car: you can either shell out a load of cash on a flashy BMW that plenty of people will look at as you ride around; or rather less on a smaller model that you don't mind getting a few dents in on your first road trip. Either way, you're going to have to do the driving so go with what you feel most comfortable in.

 **LAURA**

Taking the plunge: Learning to swim

When I was about five, I used to like swimming. My mum tells me that I used to swim quite happily as long as I couldn't touch the bottom. I liked the deep end. Then I didn't go swimming for a long while and seemingly forgot how (or at least lost the confidence) to swim. Undeterred, I would splash around quite happily in the shallow end, until one day when I was about eight. I'd gone swimming with my friend, Annie, and her older sister. I jumped into the pool where the water was deeper than I'd expected. My feet reached out for the bottom but it was too far away and I swallowed mouthfuls of water as I panicked and tried to keep above the surface. The lifeguard extended a long pole towards me and I grabbed hold of one end as he hoisted me out. I remember sitting by the side of the pool next to the lifeguard, catching my breath, feeling embarrassed and scared.

Deciding to do my first triathlon meant getting better at swimming. I only swam when I was on holiday, so that was a total of about 10 hours swimming in the past three years. And that wasn't so much swimming as paddling in slightly deeper water. I didn't need to consult Katie to know that this was short of the amount recommended by most triathlon training schedules.

I told people I was having lessons because I needed to 'get better at swimming' but what I really meant was 'learn to swim', because what I did when submerged in water was not so much swimming as trying not to drown. I couldn't put my face in the water because the chlorine would burn my nostrils and so, when trying to do front crawl, I'd turn my head from side to side above the water, thrashing about wildly with my arms and kicking my legs awkwardly beneath me. There was a lot of movement going on, but none of it seemed to be pushing me forwards particularly quickly. My breaststroke was even worse; I almost went backwards. When I finally did make it to the other end of the pool, I was so worn out I'd have to have a long rest before swimming back. I'd run several marathons without stopping and yet swimming 50 metres in one go was beyond me.

I took baby steps towards becoming a better swimmer. I purchased a one-piece swimsuit for the first time since I was 13 and headed off to a lake. This was a decision prompted more by the unseasonably hot April back in 2011 than any thought out training regime. It was a Saturday morning and I was determined not to cave and be the first person to say, 'It's too hot'. Not in April. Without air-con I had two options: spend my Saturday in the freezer section of a local supermarket or find some water to jump in. In London's Hyde Park sits the Serpentine: a big old lake that has a roped-off swimming section and which played host to the open-water swim and triathlon events at the London Olympics. Every

Christmas Day, a group of hardy swimmers enter the water to compete for the Peter Pan Cup: a 100 yard handicapped race. The Serpentine, I had decided, was the only thing that was going to stop me feeling like I was taking part in the Death Valley Ultramarathon. I hatched a plan to get on my bike and cycle the 8 miles there for a swim. After 8 miles of cycling on the hot London streets, my transition from bike to swim was faster than I've ever seen a pro go from swim to bike. Unfortunately, the swimming technique that followed was more iron leg than ironman. The water was cold and gave me quite a shock. While the rest of my body got used to it, my skinny little arms were pathetic and wouldn't work properly. I wasn't a swimming coach but even I knew that arms are quite important in stopping you from drowning. After a mild panic that I was, in fact, going to drown, another swimmer demonstrated a key skill for surviving in water – standing up. After I'd mastered that and calmed down I began my swim. I told myself that the things floating past my face were 'just leaves' and kept my lips tightly shut.

I thrashed about with all the grace of a wardrobe and managed 50 m. It was enough to cool me down and tick 'Swimming in the Serpentine' off my list of things to do. But it was also enough to confirm that I wouldn't become a triathlete any time soon. My one-piece swimsuit went back in the cupboard where it stayed for more than a year. I just wasn't meant to be good at swimming.

I spent Christmas Day that year, not competing for the Peter Pan Cup, but on a beach in Australia. I have a photo of me splashing about in the water wearing a Santa hat. I'd been to Sydney where the outdoor swimming pools sparkled in the heat of the day and tried to entice me in. I did a couple of lengths in a deserted pool in a small town called Bellingen, New South Wales but got out when some children who'd barely mastered walking got in and put my swimming to shame. I had a surfing lesson in a town called 1770 – the photo of me stood up on the board looks quite impressive until you notice the instructor stood behind me, the water only up to his chest. My lack of swimming skills wasn't stopping me doing things, but it was limiting my enjoyment of them. I went to the Great Barrier Reef, where I went snorkelling with a life jacket tightly fastened round my chest; and when I went on a boat trip a few weeks later in Cambodia, and the sea on the way back became a bit choppy, I'd already counted the number of people on board and the number of life jackets and discreetly dragged one over with my foot ready to put on. Learning to swim wasn't something that I should be doing for the sake of a triathlon; it's an essential life skill.

Trying to learn to swim from a book isn't the best idea in the world. For a start the pages get all soggy. But this was how I resumed my quest to swim properly. I armed myself with a copy of *Total Immersion*, got myself a pair of goggles and a nose clip, and gave up all hope of ever having nice hair again. I was ready to become a swimmer. After reading three chapters, I was all set to dip my toe into the world of swim training. The book attempts to teach swimming in a similar manner to which martial arts is taught – by only letting you do one small component at a time and making you practise it over and over before you can move on to the next. Coincidentally, I'd waxed on and waxed off before I headed to the pool for my first session.

My first swim consisted of floating on my back with my arms by my sides, swimming a length like that, and then floating on each side with my arms by my sides and swimming a length like that. The grand finale was a length floating on each side for a few seconds before switching to the other side and then repeating. Despite the pool not being very busy, I felt hugely self-conscious, and not because of the unflattering one-piece bathing suit, nose clip and goggles combo. I'd forgotten what it felt like in those early days of starting running – I remembered the pain and exhaustion of trying to run for 5 minutes non-stop, but had forgotten how convinced I was that everyone was looking at me and judging me.

I got a few puzzled looks from the locals at the pool in Tower Hamlets, East London but my early swims went OK as far as I could tell. But without someone saying, 'Yes, that's right' or 'No, just no!' I was a bit lost as to how well it was really going. So after a few weeks of not moving past chapter three, in August 2012, I booked myself onto an eight-week swim course and turned up 40 minutes early for the first lesson that I hoped would transform me, if not quite into Rebecca Adlington, then into a swimmer that less resembled a wardrobe.

I'd never been able to keep water out of my nose and, on holidays, I would dive into water headfirst but holding my nose, much to the amusement of my family. I'd seen one of the American swimmers win gold in the Olympics wearing a nose clip and he revealed in a post-race interview that he too couldn't keep water out of his nostrils. This cheered me. I was closer to being an Olympic swimmer than I'd thought. I told this story to the swim coach at the start of my first lesson as I fixed my clip and got ready to jump into the pool. Her response: 'That's nice. But you won't be wearing that in these lessons.' What? No nose clip? She had a firm manner that wasn't to be argued with, so I didn't question why, I just reluctantly discarded it and got on with the first task: sitting on the bottom and blowing bubbles. And it turned out I didn't die and the water stayed in the pool where it was supposed to be. The lesson continued and there were a few brain-stinging moments when I forgot to breathe out and the chlorine found its way into places it shouldn't be, but in the main it went OK. It was a small step, but shedding the nose clip was a big achievement for me.

Each week, the three other people on my course and I were taught some drills by our slightly eccentric coach that we'd then have to go away and practise. They all had interesting names like the 'Polar Bear' and 'Tickle, itch, salute'. There were weeks when I expected a camera crew to jump out from behind the diving board and shout, 'Ha ha, we're just joking with you!' But I went along with it.

'Open your mouth under the water and let the water in.' This was her advice one week for stopping us swallowing pool water. I was slightly worried that she was trying to kill me. I'd rather not drink my own bathwater let alone water that a good hundred people have been splashing around in. It seems counter-intuitive – stop drinking the swimming pool by opening your mouth and letting your mouth fill with the stuff. But, as she explained, 'You need to get used to having water in your mouth, so you stop swallowing it.'

So, as well as doing an impression of a polar bear down at my local pool twice a week, I now had to imitate a basking shark too. Like a basking shark, I also caused looks of concern from the nearby lifeguards as I thrashed about, mouth wide open in the shallows – but me and a basking shark both pose no danger to other swimmers, only to ourselves.

My swim coach had been right about everything so far. I didn't need the nose clip, eventually I did stop sinking and I stopped swallowing water too. So I trusted her when she said to be patient and it would happen. To 'abandon hope but keep the faith' and the strange swimming drills, slowly but surely started to work.

At the start of October 2012, eight weeks after starting the course, she shook my hand and said: 'Congratulations, you're ready for the advanced class.' I'd just swum two lengths of face-in-the-water, no-nose-clip front crawl. My stroke was still shaky and I was exhausted at the end of each length, but I'd done it. This was the test that needed to be completed before I could go any further. It was just 50 metres in total but I was as happy as if I'd just swum the English Channel.

Maybe this triathlon business wasn't so far out of my grasp after all. I asked my coach when I might be ready for a sprint distance triathlon, to which she said very matter-of-factly, 'You'll be able to do one in about six to eight weeks. Olympic distance next summer and then you'll be ready for a half ironman next autumn.' My 50 metres of front crawl seemed quite far off the 1,900 m needed for a half ironman, and that wasn't even taking into account the bike or run legs. Shortly after this conversation I nearly passed out in the pool. The water was freezing that week. A sign at reception informed swimmers that, due to a problem with the heating, the pool temperature was 'cooler than usual'. It was more like an impromptu open-water swim session, but without the wetsuits. I started to feel dizzy and had to sit on the side for a few minutes before completing my last two lengths, fearful that the lifeguard would have to get his uniform wet saving me. But my coach was confident about her skill as a teacher, if not mine as a swimmer and hadn't been wrong yet. So, after I'd recovered, I let myself check out a few races. Just for research purposes.

Heading to the swimming pool after work on a Tuesday night, getting changed into my swimming costume, cap and goggles and flopping into the water gradually became second nature. Where once I dipped my toes into the cool water and lowered myself in slowly, pausing to double check my goggles and cap before I couldn't put it off any longer and submerged my shoulders – now I jumped straight in and dived below the surface. I would now swim back and forth in the pool with a steady stream of bubbles flowing from my nose with no concern for whether the odd bit of chlorinated water made its way up there too. My stroke had improved. I may not have been entirely 'slippery and fish-like' but I looked more like I was swimming not drowning and, very occasionally, it felt like I was gliding through the water rather than fighting it. Every Tuesday, after my lesson, I would get on the Tube with wet hair, eat a sandwich, and try to shake the water out of my ears. Often I'd read a book on the way home. This Tuesday evening was no different, other than that I'd just swum 1,500 m for the first time during the course of the session.

'That's an Olympic tri swim!' I said to my coach after she'd added up my lengths.

'So it is.'

I headed off for a hot shower, excited at what I'd just done. It was another milestone reached. There'd been lots of stopping at either end of the pool to catch my breath, but I'd just swum as far as I'd needed to swim for an Olympic distance triathlon. I was grinning as I got on the Tube, ate my sandwich (prawn, much to the displeasure of my fellow passengers), and reached into my bag for a book. This week's reading of choice was *A Life Without Limits*, the book Chrissie Wellington had signed a few months earlier for me. Inside the front cover, staring up at me was the message she'd written before I'd even had one swimming lesson: 'Never give up. You promised me.' And so, buoyed by a possible over-calculation of my swim distance, and encouraged by the four-time Ironman World Champion, I signed up for a half-iron distance triathlon, reassuringly called 'The Gauntlet' the following September. Yes, I hadn't swum outside at this point, let alone completed a sprint or Olympic triathlon, but I had a promise to keep.

KATIE

A splash course:
Getting back into the water

'Turn around!' the teacher shouted from the side. 'Turn around!'

I must have been five or six years old and learning to swim in the kids' pool. Without the opportunity themselves, my parents grew up as non-swimmers and they were keen to breed three fish. They plopped my brothers and me into lessons and swimming club as soon as they knew we could float. I was puzzled by the teacher's instructions and just couldn't see how turning around would help me swim this so-called 'backstroke'. Surely that would put me on my front again and facing the bottom? Didn't she know anything?

'Turn around!' she shouted again.

'But why?' I spluttered back.

'Your head is touching the wall!'

I love swimming now but it hasn't always come easily. Whether it's from bad memories of swimming lessons as a kid, a fear of water, a lack of opportunity, or because a soggy plaster once floated up your nose, there are plenty of reasons that people come to triathlon with a gap in their swimming CV, and a challenge to overcome in just getting to the start line of their event. If you can relate to any of these, it's important to allow yourself the time to build your swim confidence and, for that reason, we're putting this chapter early on in this book so that you can find out what you need to know and where to start with swimming for a triathlon.

In the swim

The swim in a triathlon takes place either in a pool (indoor or outdoor) or in the open water (lake, river or sea). A pool triathlon is a great place to start if you are relatively new to swimming, or less confident in the water, since the ends and the bottom of the pool are both kept in sight and offer the security of somewhere to pause if necessary. There are two common formats for a triathlon with a pool swim:

1. Small swim 'waves', where a few people are set off a few seconds apart to complete the distance in the same lane; this requires a reasonably accurate (honest) swim prediction time when you enter the race so that you are grouped with people of similar speeds, and avoid too much overtaking and congestion in the lane. For me, the biggest problem with this set-up is having to count my laps; I find this tricky enough in training, never mind when I'm racing. At least at my first triathlon, I was told in the race briefing, 'Don't worry if you lose count, when you've swum 28 lengths, someone will put a big number two in the water.' Luckily,

it was just a laminated sign with a numeral on it; I kept my mouth closed in the shallow end just in case.

2. A 'procession'-style time trial sees swimmers setting off at larger intervals (e.g. a minute) between. Often this involves swimming up and down each lane before moving across the pool a lane at a time. If that's hard to visualise, picture someone mowing stripes into a lawn and you're not too far from the idea. A marshal will be happy to talk you through this before you swim. You'll have to duck under the lane rope each time you switch lanes, but there's less need for counting, or threats of a number two.

Open-water swims vary more in terms of the length of the course but typically involve a route marked out by buoys and one or more laps of the course. Other differences include the strength and direction of current (in river and sea swims) and the salinity of the water (the presence of salt will increase buoyancy in sea water); weather conditions will also affect the temperature and how calm or wavy the water is. Whether taking place in a river, lake or the sea, a distinctive feature of an open-water swim is the 'mass start' where a large wave of swimmers begin their race at the same time. The Ironman races can have more than a thousand swimmers starting at once, a smaller race might have a wave of 50–100 people. It's an exhilarating experience but one that requires some confidence in the water.

Different strokes

A question often asked is, 'Do I have to swim front crawl?' The rules of the International Triathlon Union state that competitors, 'May use any stroke to propel themselves through the water. They may also tread water or float.' The latter part of which seems obvious but it does allow you the opportunity to pause and take a rest if needed. You'll see most triathletes swim front crawl; it's a relatively efficient stroke and saves your legs for what's to come after the swim.

Some people will swim breaststroke and many find it helpful to break up an open-water swim and check that they are swimming in the right direction. If you are planning to swim in open water, it's worth remembering that wetsuits aren't designed with breaststroke in mind so it isn't recommended to cover the whole course doing this stroke. Although the official rules allow it, some organisers ask that competitors don't swim backstroke since it can be confused with a distress signal in open water, though if you're making reasonable progress in a forwards direction then that should lessen the confusion. (Perhaps these organisers once witnessed a six-year-old girl swimming backstroke in a pool in Hereford in the 1980s and promptly adopted a 'one size fits all' rule?) If you're considering swimming butterfly for your first triathlon then you may wish to skip this chapter, or at least be aware that, in terms of etiquette, it is the equivalent of licking a yoghurt lid in front of your nan.

Lessons learned

If you are starting from scratch as a swimmer, swimming lessons will be a great investment. Contact your local pool to ask about adult swimming lessons and be sure to tell the instructor about what you are hoping to achieve. Triathlon is a sport on the up and many people are learning to swim as adults with a triathlon specifically in mind. There are several swim coaching companies helping to help get adults swimming, many with a focus on triathlon: Swim for Tri is just one example of a London-based coaching company, and Swim Smooth has coaches around the UK, offering one-to-one video analysis, coaching clinics, and DVDs (though watching them in the pool is tricky). Swim Smooth also wrote the swim coaching curriculum for British Triathlon so their style will be consistent with the coaching at your local triathlon club, if and when you decide to join.

If you think you're too old to learn, think again. My mum took adult swimming lessons in her 40s so that she could take up triathlon. Better still, I once met a chap called Ken on a swimming holiday: he was 78 and had been a surfer all his life but decided to learn to swim properly when he was 70. He was resistant to lessons so, instead, he said he took coaching advice over the phone from an old university friend. He also told me that he once saw a sea monster the size of a St Bernard swimming next to his surf board, so believe what you like about his swimming story. What remains true is that he completed every swim on the trip and had to be talked down from doing a handstand on the side of the boat during a lunchtime diving competition. If we could all guarantee being like Ken at the tender age of 78 then I think more people would take up swimming.

When you start your lessons, be open and honest with your teacher about your experience and, if relevant, tell them of any fears or concerns. For many people, their feelings about water can go back a long way. My boyfriend is happy enough in water but he spends most of the time under it. Delving a little deeper, I found out that his dad learned to swim attached to the end of a rope in Bridport Harbour. A small lad, he spent half of his time completely submerged, half of his time entirely out of the water. Is it any wonder that a love of swimming wasn't passed on through the generations? A good teacher will listen to you, find out what has been holding you back until now, and take this into consideration in your lessons.

Your teacher will take you through all the steps needed to build your confidence and turn you into a barracuda, but there are also plenty of things that you can do as homework to help you feel at home in the water. Start with submerging your face and blowing bubbles through your mouth and nose, then move onto playing games, sinking to the bottom, picking things up, doing handstands, jumping off the side, do anything that makes you smile. Just remember to follow the rules of the pool: as the sign says, 'no ducking, no smoking, no petting'. The key is to become happy in the water, to spend time in the water and learn to love it. When you're comfortable, sink quietly to the bottom of the pool and spend a moment looking around and realising how tranquil it all is underwater, then bob merrily to the surface and revel in the beautiful weightlessness of it all (something certainly to be enjoyed if you spend any time running).

Breathe easy

Expect to learn a lot about breathing as you become a swimmer. With it being a fundamental process for survival, and having some obvious barriers where water is involved, a lot of people say this is the bit they find trickiest. Interestingly, most people worry about inhaling; it's only natural but rest assured that you'll find this bit easy as long as you remember only to do it when your mouth is out of the water. The secret you'll learn is that becoming a swimmer is all about breathing out. Exhaling is really important. In fact, I've heard it said that you should always be exhaling when you're swimming, and the only time you're not is when you are inhaling. The reasons for this are twofold: firstly, exhaling properly helps to maintain your body position in the water. Sinking legs are a common complaint amongst triathletes and the problem is only exacerbated if you're clinging onto a lungful of air like a life raft. Secondly, breathing out is what expels carbon dioxide, a waste product of all the lovely work your muscles are doing while swimming, and this prevents it building up in your blood stream. Carbon dioxide concentration is the stimulus in your body that causes your breathing rate to increase, not a lack of oxygen. The more carbon dioxide there is, the more your body feels it needs to breathe, which is what can lead to that panicky feeling underwater. So breathing out helps to maintain a feeling of relaxation, which is exactly what you want. Try it now: take a big breath in, and let a stonking great big sigh of a breath out. Feel better? Or just a bit self-conscious because you did that on a packed commuter train? If you do any yoga then you'll know that the focus is on the breathing and that the exhalation is where the body relaxes; the bonus in swimming is that, unlike in yoga class, if you fart while you're doing it, no one will really notice.

A fresh start

It's funny that my earliest memory of swimming should be a backstroke blunder, since I think that's what triggered the end of my swimming club career a few years later too. Being asked to demonstrate in front of the other kids was the greatest accolade going and one rarely bestowed upon me. I beamed with pride when I was asked to swim a length while the others looked on. As I emerged from the water, waiting to hear a detailed debrief on my technical proficiency, our coach uttered, 'And, that's how not to do it.'

Even facing the right way, it seemed my backstroke still wasn't up to scratch. So, shortly after, a crestfallen teenage girl decided to pursue interests other than swimming. However bruised my ego, I knew I was fortunate to have spent so long growing up with a permanently faint whiff of chlorine in my hair and I found my underwater background very useful when I started to dabble in a couple of triathlons in my twenties. Although zipping up a wetsuit and swimming in a lake was a whole new experience, the swimming itself didn't pose too much of a concern and I got by without any real swim preparation, but the lack of training showed. Many former swimmers find their way back into swimming later on, perhaps burned out from too much time staring at the tiled black line, and it's not so much a new skill to be learned but a new take on the sport that's needed to reignite your interest.

My motivation remained at large until three years later when a friend suggested we go on a swimming holiday with the company, SwimTrek. I had a new job with a pool on site and my local triathlon club trained there, leaving me with no excuse not to get back in the water. Slipping into the shallow end of a lane, hoping I could keep up with those around me, I remember feeling a bit self-conscious introducing myself to other people with less than a millimetre of fabric between us and total nudity; I felt like an awkward teenager again and got through my training sessions with the same shyness. Still, with every winter session completed, the summer holiday on Croatia's Dalmatian coast grew closer. That first holiday had me hooked on open water and helped to turn me into the born-again swimmer I am today. Swimming outside is like swimming in 3D for your senses: the colours that take you beyond the black line along the bottom; the sunlight that shatters as it hits the water like a prism; and swimming through the temperature fluctuations that are certainly less worrying than those you experience in the pool. Behind all of that is a community of open-water swimmers who are some of the friendliest, most enthusiastic and inclusive people you will meet in sport. The sport of open-water swimming is booming in the UK at the moment and, regardless of your triathlon ambitions, giving this a try might be just what you need to reignite your enthusiasm for swimming. I know that whenever I'm swimming backstroke badly on a dark, winter night in the pool, I think of when I'll next be back swimming in 3D.

If you're already a competent and motivated swimmer then I'm afraid you may have gained little in the way of practical advice in this chapter. I hope you will, at least, arrive at the start of your first triathlon with an appreciation of what some people have achieved to make it there; those people for whom confidence in the water is not something that they've ever taken for granted. We all have to learn somewhere. I may have learned as a kid, but there were times when I found it confusing and frustrating; I'm telling you this now because, if you're learning to swim then it might seem scary and insurmountable. Whenever you do it, learning to swim is a big deal but it is definitely worth persevering. As Laura said, swimming is not only a prerequisite for triathlon but it's a life skill. Stick with it because you are learning to do something very special indeed.

The perfect storm: Swimming in open water

> The lake is open but likely to be a bit choppy. It'll be fine but just to warn you: good race practice! K x

I checked the weather forecast for the evening – 22 mph winds and some rain. This was weather meant for staying indoors, lighting a fire and having a dog curl up on your lap. But as I had my first sprint triathlon to do in ten days' time, and as I didn't have a fire or a dog, I had no excuse not to put on a wetsuit and jump in a lake.

While I'd swum as much as 1,500 metres in the pool by this point, I would still regularly stop at the end of a length. Sometimes there'd be someone waiting to set off and it was polite to wait for them, sometimes I had to empty water out of my goggles, and sometimes these were excuses because I didn't think I could keep going. I stopped at the end of my lengths because I thought I needed to – to catch my breath, have a rest, or because I thought my lungs would burst if I didn't grab onto the side of the pool and stop for a few seconds.

I'd gone to the pool after work one day and, as I was swimming along, I swallowed some water. I rolled onto my back to cough it up before I started going again. In that brief pause the swimmer behind me (who was swimming on his back) started to swim into me. I ducked under the water and briefly panicked. I panicked because it was unexpected, it hadn't happened before, and because it was at a point in the pool where I couldn't reach the bottom or the sides. I fumbled my way to the surface and recovered, coughed some more, and was soon on my way swimming the rest of my length.

I carried on swimming, thinking about my unexpected dunk. What would I do if this happened in a race, in open water, where the sides are even further away? I didn't want to go through that. I couldn't do it. I couldn't swim 750 metres in a river. But I carried on swimming. I'd now swum 600 metres up and down the pool with a rest every couple of lengths. I had panicked for the same reason that I kept stopping at the end of lengths: because I still saw myself as a non-swimmer. I stopped one last time, adjusted my goggles, shook the water out of my ears, and waited for the person in front of me to push off. Then I did the same. I pushed off from the wall and I swam up and down the lane, and I didn't stop until I'd swum ten lengths, totalling 300 metres. And it felt great. I wasn't a non-swimmer any more. I was a swimmer. Now I just had to become the sort of swimmer that swam in rivers.

I shared my concerns about just how badly my first sprint triathlon was going to go with my boyfriend, Phil. His response: 'You'll probably be really rubbish at it. But at least it will be funny.' Funny for who though? With just two weeks to go until the race, Phil and I headed to the swimming ponds on Hampstead Heath, where the chalkboard said the water was a crisp 13°C but my toes said otherwise. I had a wetsuit, my companion did not – who's laughing now? There was a group of people standing around the water, daring each other to jump in, threatening to push each other in, and testing the water with their toes before shaking their heads and staring at the water some more. I wriggled into my newly acquired wetsuit, ready for its maiden voyage, and felt like the only person at a party who has turned up in fancy dress. I hadn't got the last minute text that the Batman theme had been cancelled. Turning up to swim in a wetsuit at Hampstead Heath felt rather like turning up to a bowling alley with your own ball or going ice skating with your own skates. It sets a certain level of expectation among those watching that you know what you're doing. The pressure to get a strike or skate backwards was on as I headed towards the water when all I was trying to do was avoid getting a verruca or wart.

I put my feet in. It was cold. Swimmers wearing just a small piece of Lycra swam past. I had to get in. The initial coldness of the water on my feet didn't go away like it does in the pool, the only way to warm them up was to get in and start moving. I lowered my legs in, then my body, and pushed away from the steps. My body didn't feel cold, the wetsuit kept me warm and, more importantly for this scared swimmer, made me float. I bobbed about in the water for a while wondering if I could get a cocktail and just float there all afternoon. But the lifeguard had asked that I keep to the back of the swimming area as I was in a wetsuit (and he'd wrongly assumed I would be doing some sort of speedy swimming up and down) so I rolled onto my stomach ready to swim up there. I put my face into the water and gasped from the cold, inhaling a lungful of pond water. Breathing was proving difficult so I ambled my way through the water with my face up. It took another 5 minutes before I could put my face down and do something my swim coach might recognise – but the water was dark and I couldn't see where I was going and so I swam in big curves. After 10 minutes, I gave up and headed, in a zigzag fashion, back to the steps. I didn't feel confident about my upcoming triathlon.

Katie had offered to take me open-water swimming two years before when I first voiced my intention to become a triathlete. But this was before I'd learnt how to swim or she'd fully comprehended just how much of a non-swimmer I was. I didn't think she'd go for my suggestion of towing me round on a lilo so I decided to learn how to swim first. My sprint triathlon debut was now just ten days away and the fact that I had to swim 750 metres in a river was scaring the life out of me. So I took her up on the offer. We met at Bray Lake – a location equally inconvenient for both of us sitting halfway between our respective homes in North London and Oxford, while being easily accessible from neither. But the cheery guys down at the lake made the trip worthwhile and they weren't deterred by the weather. There was a friendly community feel to the lake – people were swimming together in groups and telling us, 'It's not so bad once you're in.'

We paid our money and were handed a brightly coloured swim hat each and pointed in the direction of the lake. A lake where two renegades were swimming about in just their trunks. Everyone else was zipped up tightly in a wetsuit – there was none of the odd-one-out embarrassment I'd experienced at Hampstead Heath. This time, calmly talked through it all by Katie, who I considered my own personal lifesaver and cheerleader, I was in the water and face down (in a good way) quicker than last time. We swam a 400 m loop out across the lake and around some marker buoys while the wind picked up the water and smacked it in our faces every time we lifted them to breathe.

The last 50 metres of the loop was headfirst into the wind. I had to stop every 10 metres to catch my breath – it turns out you don't need the end of a swimming pool lane to do this. Katie assured me I was 'doing great' and, after what seemed an eternity, we made it back to the start. I left Katie to swim a second lap by herself while I watched on from the deck. As I sat there, another pair of women approached the ladder. One said to the other, 'I can't believe it's so windy for your first open-water swim. Honestly, it's not usually like this. If you can swim in this though, you can swim in anything.'

I watched Katie glide round the marker buoys. Swimming in a big lake or a river made sense to me only when I compared it to the differences of running on the treadmill and running outside. It's scary at first and it's more difficult than logic tells you it should be. To begin with, you're concentrating so hard on putting one foot in front of the other, and not stepping in dog poo, that you can't appreciate the benefits of being outside: the fresh air, the grass, the progress. I hoped that sometime soon I'd be able to lift up my head while swimming and look at what was around me. What had started off as a mission to be able to swim a mile in a lake by September had changed. It had now become a plan to learn how to love swimming outside the way that Katie did. It might take more time than the original plan, but I was sure it would be more rewarding in the long run.

Falling in love requires a series of positive experiences, good memories that you associate with a name or a word. For a long time, when I thought about swimming I thought of damp changing rooms, wet hair on a cold walk home from the pool, and soggy towels in my bag. I thought about the sting of water going up my nose, being pulled out of the pool by a lifeguard, coughing and spluttering on the side, embarrassed and scared. Of being starving as soon as I got out of the water and buying salt and vinegar crisps from the vending machine. Of summers at the local lido as a teenager where dead flies and plasters floated past on water so cold it took all day to get in. With those ideas in my head of what swimming meant, and in spite of many of them, I had headed to my first swimming lesson. I wanted to learn how to swim properly so that I could complete a triathlon. I hadn't gone to the pool expecting to learn to love swimming, but slowly, that's what happened.

As my love for swimming grew, I started to explore new territories. I swam in a different pool; one recently restored to its Victorian splendour with a vaulted glass ceiling and (on one Saturday afternoon) jazz musicians playing from the viewing area above. I swam in a bright blue saltwater lake in Croatia, swimming up and down watching fish underneath me going about their fishy business. I spent an evening bobbing about in a wetsuit in the middle of a cold lake while it blew a gale but felt safe knowing that the wetsuit and my companion wouldn't let there be a repeat of that coughing and spluttering lifeguard rescue of 20 years earlier.

Not so long ago I couldn't swim, and now I can swim in lakes and rivers without feeling scared. That's what I think about now when I think about swimming. And in time, I did learn to love it.

Outdoors and in rubber:
A guide to open-water swimming

I was never in any doubt that Laura would turn up to swim in that gale. This is Laura we're talking about. I knew that she would get in and swim. This is Laura. What I wasn't sure about was whether she would ever want to go swimming in open water again. This is an obvious concern when your friend's first open-water triathlon is on the horizon and you have had the bright idea of suggesting she try it out on one of the most miserable evenings ever seen in the month of May. Something I also knew was that if I wasn't meeting her that evening, then I probably wouldn't have gone swimming in a lake in that weather. No, I would have been tucked up at home, listening to the rain hammer down on the window panes as I sipped a nice, hot cup of tea. For that, Laura has more of my respect than I can possibly put into words. I love swimming outdoors, and I wanted my friend to love it too; there are nicer ways of getting into it than the way Laura experienced it, and if she can turn around and say she loved it, then I'm confident that you can be converted too.

In its most basic terms, open-water swimming involves swimming outside the confines of a pool. In a triathlon, it can take the form of a lake, river or sea swim, but the open swimming world extends well beyond the sport of triathlon and there are lots of ways to experience its glory: from the moonlit wild swims of the Outdoor Swimming Society; to holidays in beautiful waters around the world; and designated open-water swimming events, such as the Great North Swim or the Henley Swim races. In fact, I'd recommend you try any of the above to get in and have a go, even if a triathlon didn't feature on your 'To Do' list. There are books dedicated to finding secluded spots around the country where you can take a dip, such as *Wild Swimming* by Daniel Start, *Wild Swim* by Kate Rew, and Roger Deakin's wild swimming journey across Britain, *Waterlog*. I would always recommend that you go along with someone else: I'm all for adventure but with open-water swimming there has to be a sensible balance between guts and common sense. Recognising the growing demand of more adventurous swimmers, there are clubs popping up around the UK; more and more water sports lakes are also opening up designated open-water swimming centres offering opportunities for swimmers to use the lakes with safety support, and, if you are very lucky, bacon butties sizzling away on the barbecue for when you get out.

Suit yourself

If an open-water triathlon in the UK is on your horizon, then you're going to need a wetsuit. Swimming wetsuits differ from surfing wetsuits in terms of the flexibility and the thickness of the neoprene material used: a surfing wetsuit will get you through an open-water swim but a swimming wetsuit will be designed to offer more comfort and better performance thanks to the distribution of buoyancy and reduction of drag. Wetsuit sizing can be a slightly tricky business: too big and it'll fill up with water and slow you down; too small and you'll find out how the Angel of the North would feel trying to swim freestyle. By way of a simple size guide: it's not uncommon that the right size of wetsuit would require a little additional help doing up the zip at the back. A lovely moment of solidarity can be seen at the start of events where total strangers turn to each other and say, 'Do me up, will you?' If you're able to manage the zip with too much ease by yourself, you could probably afford to consider a smaller suit; if it takes two or more pairs of hands to hold you down and force the zip closed, I'd argue that you've gone a size too small. While there's no real substitute for trying on a suit first, I bought my first swimming wetsuit online after a little research and it served me well for several years. There are also hire options available if you want to try out a suit for a season before committing. All manufacturers will have a size guide on their website and it's generally recommended to follow their weight guides as much as their dimensions when choosing your size.

Greased lightning

If you're going to pour yourself into this rubber suit, you're going to need a little something extra to help you in and out. Lubrication is a common sight among any group of people struggling into their swimming wetsuits; it has the additional benefit of protecting you from any rubbing at the neck or seams, particularly under the arm, as you swim. Choosing the right substance is a matter of much debate. Never be tempted to consider talcum powder to ease your way; it might have helped to get your socks back on after swimming in PE, but once you're in the water, it'll mix up like plaster of Paris and leave you cast into a permanent front crawl position. While Vaseline seems to be the obvious choice, the Internet scaremongers would have it that such petroleum-based products will munch through your wetsuit like moths, rendering it completely unusable. I haven't seen any solid evidence that supports this claim of rampant chemical destruction and would assume that it would only cause significant problems if you kept your wetsuit for 100 years (by which time, you might be grateful for the extra slack that this would afford when getting into it) but I've still never taken the chance and prefer to use one of the alternatives available just in case.

Body Glide is a brand commonly recommended by water sports enthusiasts, it also comes in a handy roll-on form so you can retain some purchase on the container even in your most slippery state. I've always been a bit of a baby oil fan myself, mostly because it makes your legs look all shiny afterwards. I dare say anything slippery would probably do the job though I've yet to see anyone dressing themselves in extra virgin olive oil at a race; then again, maybe the triathlons I'm entering aren't expensive enough. If none of those do it for you, Laura and I did receive rave reviews from a lady we chatted to in the changing tent at an open-water swim event; smothering herself in Durex Play, we assumed she was talking about putting her wetsuit on but, just in case, we reminded her of those pool rules we discussed earlier, 'no ducking, no smoking, no petting'.

Whatever coating you choose, put plenty around your ankles and wrists before putting the suit on and that should help later with taking it off; something you'll be doing at speed before getting on your bike. Also, apply a decent smear around your neck and anywhere else you're worried about chafing, and give your hands a good clean before going anywhere near your goggles.

Zip code

Now you're ready to put the suit on, which is arguably one of the more exhausting parts of a day out at a triathlon, and definitely something that will make you glad that the swim is first. First things first: the zip goes at the back. I repeat: the zip goes at the back. Remove any jewellery, since necklaces can rub and rings can become loose in cold water, and make sure that your nails are free of any sharp edges so that you don't damage the suit. One foot at a time, roll up the legs of the suit like you're putting on a pair of tights.

Some people put carrier bags on their feet to help free them from the legs; if you do this, one of those flimsy supermarket ones is best, not a hessian 'bag for life' (or you'll be there a lifetime trying to escape the lower regions of your wetsuit), and remember to take the bags off before you go swimming. Gently pull the suit up, bit by bit, over your knees and stand for a moment, triumphantly, with your hands on your hips, looking down at what you have achieved.

Next up, the thighs present the difficult step and it's important to tackle this with confidence – never let your wetsuit sense your fear. Success in this stage is achieved in a number of ways: I try to pull up as much of the leg as I can, then follows a less dignified version of the River Dance while I try to coax the suit up somewhere towards my backside. Do what you need to do. No one is judging you. Wetsuit adornment is not a spectator sport and all participants follow a silent code of mutual ignorance at the rubbery struggling going on around them.

Gently pinching the suit with the fleshy pads of your fingers (not your fingernails) will help to move the neoprene against your skin and edge the legs of the suit ever closer to their ultimate destination: as close to your crotch as you can possibly get them. Now up to your waist in neoprene, you may turn around and see someone release a sigh of enormous disappointment having realised that they have their zip at the front. You won't be that person. If you see this happen, look at the floor, fiddle with the brakes on your bike, pretend there's something in your eye, anything to avoid letting them know that you know. They will feel bad enough as it is. And if this is you, rest assured that this, like losing your house keys or eating yellow snow, is a mistake you will only make once.

The next stages are now relatively straightforward: as with the legs, gently does it putting your arms in one at a time (the carrier bags on the hands work well again here); spend some time pulling the arms up sufficiently around the shoulders to give you a good range of movement and a chance in hell of the zip meeting at the back, and check that the armpits are flush with yours. Then, find a friend (or make a new one), breathe out, draw your shoulders back and ask them to zip you up, checking that the flap of neoprene behind the zip is lying nice and flat. Most suits have an extra Velcro fastening at the top and a long zip cord that you will need to find as you leave the swim so that you can release yourself from the suit; while your buddy is still there, check that you are able to find the cord and undo the suit. This whole process can be hot and sweaty so, on race day, leave plenty of time before the start of your wave to do this; if it's a warm day, you can put the suit on as far as your waist and wait to finish the top half on your way down to the swim. I know that I like to leave doing that zip up as long as I possibly can.

Head start

With your wetsuit on, let's sort out what's on your head. Swimming hats are a must for open-water swimming, both for a bit of warmth and to be able to spot you bobbing around. Most triathlons with an open-water swim will provide a brightly coloured swimming hat to help identify you in the water, some of them are even sensible enough to provide a cap that's a different colour to the buoys you'll be trying to follow. A top tip is to wear your own hat underneath this one; not only does it help keep your head toasty, but you can put your goggles over the first hat and secure them in place with the race cap on top. If you happen to make contact with someone else during the swim then you know that your goggles aren't going to budge. Owning two swimming hats may seem excessive to new swimmers at first but you'll be glad of them in cold water; besides, after a few triathlons, your swimming kit will seem to contain enough rubber for you to fashion a small bouncy castle and hire it out for parties.

Goggles are a very personal choice; you'll see people with specialist masks for open water but I'm perfectly happy using the same ones I use in the pool. The most important thing is a good seal that will stop any water leaking in, and different styles will suit different faces. Just make sure that your swimming hat is above your goggles; trapping the edge in the seal of the goggles is a common mistake that will certainly lead to leaks and one that can be easily avoided. Despite the boldest claims and best coatings, goggles can have more of a tendency to fog up in cold water than they will in the swimming baths but, if you don't want your world to be plunged into soft focus, there are some things you can do. Splashing your face with some cold water and immersing your goggles for a few minutes as you're getting in helps to adjust them to the temperature of the water, reducing the risk of condensation. A less scientific but equally effective method is to spit into your goggles and coat the inside of the lenses, give them a rinse in the lake, and then put them on. It's not nice but it works and it's something I've done for so long now that I have a Pavlovian response whenever I'm near a large enough body of open water.

Cold comfort

When you get into the water, it's a good idea to fill the wetsuit with water by pulling gently at the neck while underwater. Water will rush in and you will shriek at first, but that layer of water will help to keep you warm, as well as help with taking the suit off quickly after the swim. When you've done that, you can adjust the shoulders again and make sure that you have plenty of movement, before squashing down the torso, arms and legs with your hands to get rid of excess water and stop your suit filling up with more water as you swim. If you're using your own suit, take this opportunity to have a widdle too. Don't be shocked. A coach once told me, 'There are two types of people in the world, Katie: those who wee in their wetsuits and liars.'

It's an important part of the temperature regulation process as your body acclimatises to the cold water. That might be a lie. It's more that the cold water shocks you into needing a tinkle and there's really no way you'll be struggling with the zip once that urge has hit home. Accept that this is an inevitable part of open-water swimming and enjoy the freedom; just avoid cleaning your goggles in the pool of water next to the competitor with a faraway look in their eyes.

Set your sights

You're in and you're ready to swim. There are two things you may have noticed by now: it's cold, and you cannot see a thing underwater. This can be the source of anxiety for many a first time open-water swimmer and this is where you remember rule number one about relaxing in water: exhaling is your friend. Even before you start to swim, take a deep breath, place your face in the water, and blow a load of bubbles out through your nose and mouth (shout, sing, say some naughty words at the same time if you like). I'm going to take a moment to tell you now that you will be just fine, and you should also take that moment to tell yourself the very same thing. If at any time you feel nervous during your swim, remember rule number one and check that you are breathing out.

During this ritual, you may also have noticed that there is no tiled black line on the bottom, which is a lovely thing really, but it does mean that you are going to have to find your way around without this guide. 'Sighting' is a key skill for open-water swimmers and one worth practising. It basically involves lifting your head up above the water frequently enough to spot a marker and check that you're on course, but not so frequently that you look like you're bobbing for apples. The 'skill' bit comes in being able to do this while you're still swimming front crawl. A triathlon swim course will generally be marked out by buoys, and the ability to sight will let you take the shortest line between them without too much zigzagging. Aim to pop your head up, facing forwards, every few strokes so that your eyes are just above the surface to check the marker and adjust your line if necessary; when you want to do this, a slightly firmer push down with your arm in the water should help raise you enough in the water and a stronger kick or two will assist. Try to avoid breathing while facing forward, instead roll your head to the side to breathe once you have looked up, and carry on swimming. If my description was as clear as the water you are trying to swim in then YouTube is useful for more than just videos of kittens on skateboards, and there are some great coaching videos that can take you through the sequence. You don't need to wait until you're out in the open to practise sighting and it's worthwhile having a go in the pool; you might feel silly at first but you'll feel sillier if you've put in all that time to get fit in the pool then paddle off in the wrong direction once you're in a lake.

Follow the crowd

The other aspect of a triathlon swim in open water that can come as a surprise is being surrounded by other swimmers; again, staying relaxed is key here. A mass start is normal in triathlon and will either take place on land, with swimmers running in like extras from *Baywatch*, or it will take place in deep water; the latter will require you to tread water for a few minutes before the start but rest assured that your wetsuit will be helping with buoyancy during this time so you can float on your belly and scull with your arms before the start.

If you're confident in the water, then you may be happy in the maelstrom of arms and legs, in which case start as far forward as is appropriate for your swim speed; if not, there is always more calm to be found at the back of the pack in a mass start. As the field spreads out, the chaos will calm down and, within a minute or two, you will have more space in which to swim. One advantage of swimming close to others is the drafting effect available in water, which will save you energy. Drafting in water can either be achieved by swimming close to the feet of the swimmer in front, or close to their side between their ankle and hips. Swimming so close to others can come at the cost of the odd bump or knock from another swimmer but stay calm and remember that it will not have been deliberate; practising in training with other swimmers, even in the pool, can help you become more used to this.

The other place where congestion becomes likely is when you turn around one of the buoys on the course (few triathlon swims will be A to B and most will involve a turn at some point); while the shortest route is closest to the buoy, if you want to avoid a game of underwater Twister then stay a bit wider and take your time. Nothing can really beat trying this before race day and triathlon clubs are a great place for some practical advice and coaching in open water; my club runs introductory lake sessions for non-members ahead of a big local triathlon so it is worth making enquiries.

If the dressing in rubber, public application of lubricant, and urinating in cold water hasn't put you off then I think that seeing the mist rising from a cool lake on a summer's morning, hearing the gentle lapping of water against the pontoon as you slide in, and experiencing the genuine enthusiasm of open-water swimmers will help you to fall in love with swimming outdoors too. It might not sound elegant but, as we will learn, there's little in triathlon that is.

LAURA

All about the bike:
Getting new wheels

To: 'Katie King'
Subject: I want to ride my purple bicycle

Exciting news – I bought a new bike! Giddy with excitement, I signed up for a cycle event. In other news, I've hurt my leg and running is a problem – hence the impulse bike purchase. Rubbish stuff.

- -

To: 'Laura Fountain'
Subject: RE: I want to ride my purple bicycle

Sorry to hear about your leg but WHAT BIKE HAVE YOU BOUGHT?!

- -

To: 'Katie King'
Subject: RE: I want to ride my purple bicycle

At the risk of sounding like I know nothing about bikes IT'S PURPLE! I hear that's how Chris Hoy chooses his bikes.

A rainy Monday lunchtime in September posed that usual dilemma faced by office workers across the world: what to get for lunch. It was a miserable day and, to cheer myself up, I made a somewhat unconventional decision to buy a bike. It wasn't as filling as a cheese sandwich, but I hoped it would last a bit longer.

The shop assistant was somewhat taken aback when, on asking me if he could help, I said, 'Yes, I'd like a bike please,' as casually as if I'd just ordered a tuna baguette. He probably gets more 'I'm just looking – leave me alone' type customers and I'm usually in this camp. But on that Monday, frustrated by the lack of running because of a problem with my leg, I decided to bite the bullet.

I already had a bike, but it wasn't very fast – or at least I wasn't very fast on it. If I was going to do a triathlon, I needed to upgrade my wheels and get a new bike. Because I'd been reliably informed that that's what triathletes do: they spend money they don't have on their sport. So I visited a cycle shop, looked at the bikes and told the shop assistant I wanted a fast one that wasn't pink.

Shopping isn't one of my strong skills. I don't enjoy the experience of wandering around looking at things and deciding which one to buy. Trying things on is tedious to me. That isn't to say that I don't like getting new things, it's just the process of acquiring them that I don't have a lot of patience with. Buying a new bike would be a similar experience.

'I like that one,' I said to the bike man.

'That's not your size. Sit on this one.'

'I don't like that one.'

'It doesn't matter, we're just seeing which size bike you need.'

After trying out a couple of bikes and determining my size, the bike man let me have my pick. He told me all sorts of things about what sort of gears they had and what make they were but I based my decision on the same two factors as picking a horse and jockey in the Grand National: the colour and the price. The one I chose wasn't in the shop in my size, so I waited impatiently for a few weeks for my shiny new purple bike to arrive from a warehouse.

I was four when I first rode a bike free from stabilisers. My dad had been running along holding onto the back of my red Raleigh Poppet while I shouted out, 'Don't let go! Don't let go!' My legs frantically going round and round on the pedals. I was scared to take the leap by myself. My mum patiently instructed me to start by bringing one pedal up to the top of its rotation and then pressing down on it with my foot as hard as I could. I did as I was told and, just like that, I was away – pedalling under my own steam. Soon, the Raleigh Poppet was outgrown and I was given a hand-me-down bike from the daughter of a friend of my parents. It was a light pinky-purple colour and of the style that I'd come to know the cool kids referred to as a 'granny basher'. I didn't care though. I cycled up and down the street where I lived and round and round the park. I rode it and rode it until eventually the three gears it had were useless and only one brake would work. I rode it until it fell apart beneath me.

Bike number three came as a Christmas present when I was ten. This was the early 1990s and the choice for any bike-conscious ten-year-old was between a mountain bike and a 'racer'. Living in the Fens, where the terrain is pancake flat, I made the obvious choice and my granny basher was succeeded by a Raleigh Cassis mountain bike. Years later, as I was cycling through London, I saw a bike exactly the same as my old Raleigh Cassis, the bike I failed my cycling proficiency test on at primary school. I wanted to stop and take a picture, and I regretted not doing so. But later that day my sister told me that my old mountain bike was still alive and well and living in her shed. Thieves had broken into that very same shed and stolen her husband's bike, but the Raleigh Cassis remained.

That was it for bikes and cycling for a good ten years, until I moved to London and needed something cheaper and more reliable than the Tube for getting around. The Cycle to Work scheme allowed me to buy a Ridgeback Comet that I named 'The Mighty'. The Mighty served me well; built like a tank, this hybrid traversed the city numerous times, bouncing through potholes and not flinching as I flung both of us up and down curbs. I hadn't even learned to change an inner-tube because The Mighty had never had a puncture and that's quite an achievement for a six-year-old bike that enjoys going off-road.

But now it was time for a new love in my life. The sexy young Spaniard that caught my attention on that rainy lunchtime, the Orbea was my first ever road bike (or racer as the ten-year-old in me still wants to call it) and it was unlike any of the bikes I'd ever ridden. It was fast, it made light work of hills, and it didn't like being told what to do – at least not by me. Sitting on it for the first few times everything seemed wrong – I was bent over with my face pointed at the floor rather than upright so I couldn't see where I was going. And the narrow wheels and drop handlebars seemed to be working together to amplify every move I made into a sudden left or right turn.

A taxi beeped at me as I wobbled my way along the road, riding it from the shop, and, shortly after, I had a near miss with a parked car. As I rode it 5 miles through London on our first journey home together, I had to learn how to ride a bike all over again. I pulled over to the side of the road to compose myself, raised up my pedal, put my foot down as hard as my mum had instructed me, and away I went, just as shakily as I had 25 years previous.

This new bike came with an added complication: clip-in pedals. The clip-in pedals came with special cycling shoes. Up until now, I was only familiar with these shoes as being the cause of the funny walk that cyclists do when they dismount and walk into a cafe to buy a cake. They have a solid sole that doesn't bend, and a fixing under the toe where the shoe attaches to the bike, which causes the wearer to walk rather strangely. For the first few weeks of our relationship, I eased myself in, cycling to and from work wearing trainers, and using the pedals like I had on my old bike without attaching myself to them. Eventually, I could put it off no longer. I put on the cycling shoes and hobbled around the flat looking like a pro cyclist. It was now time to learn how to ride a bike while my feet were welded to the pedals because this, I'd been told, would make it easier. I was sceptical to say the least. Rowers don't attach their wrists to the oars and tennis players don't tether themselves to the tennis racquet. So quite why cyclists feel the need to bond so literally with their cycle was beyond me but, in my quest to be a proper triathlete, I clipped myself to the bike.

The shoes clip onto the pedal and release with a flick of the heel outwards as though you're doing some line-dancing move. I practised clipping them in and out of the pedals a few times while propped up against a wall, before trying this new form of physical abuse while actually moving along. Several minutes of shouting at nobody other than myself, 'Why won't it work?', 'Is the pedal the right way?' and 'Is it in yet?' followed. Then it was time to push off from the wall and pedal. I managed all of 10 metres of proper, clipped-in, woman-attached-to-bike cycling before, thud. I fell off. I'd been so focused on whether my shoe was in or out that I had forgotten the need to keep a bike moving forwards in order to keep it upright. I ground to a halt and fell sideways onto the concrete. It was another rite of passage out of the way: falling off my bike could now be ticked off my list of things that stood between me and being a proper cyclist. Although it hadn't hurt, I wasn't keen to repeat it.

I cycled a few hundred metres down the road to Finsbury Park where I managed half a mile of stopping and starting, clipping and unclipping without falling off. As the sun began to go down, I felt a little more comfortable with the shoes and the bike. I continued to head out on my road bike to cycle the 5 miles each way to work and back, preferring cycling, even in the cold, rain and traffic, to getting on the Tube. Gradually, I got used to this new way of cycling. I became more comfortable leaning forward over the handlebars and became more confident zipping through town on my new bike. When I tell people that I cycle to work through Central London, passing two of the city's accident blackspots for cyclists, they furrow their brow and shake their head, 'Oh no, I couldn't cycle in London. It's too dangerous. Aren't you worried you're going to get knocked off your bike?'

I worry about a lot of things: I hate to fly because I'm convinced that every bump or noise means imminent doom, and I double and triple check I've locked the door at night. But cycling doesn't worry me. I'm well aware of the risks of cycling and, each week, I have a couple of close calls with a taxi that hasn't seen me doing a U-turn across four lanes, or a van cutting me up. The Tuesday before I was due to run the London Marathon, I cycled through Islington on my way to work. I was deliberately going slower than usual to save my legs for the race so crawled up a big hill into Highbury at a snail's pace. After the hill levelled off, I decided this would be the last cycle before Sunday's marathon. Then: BANG. I collided with a car. I remember pulling on my brakes, shouting out at the car, and thinking, shit, this is going to hurt. Then, the next thing I remember is getting up off the ground, angry, and feeling like I was going to be sick in a bush. The driver had been driving in the opposite direction to me and had turned right across my path into a side road without looking. I collided with the passenger wing. I was relieved that I was able to get back on my bike with no broken bones and just a bit of bruising.

Despite that incident, and the many near misses I've had, I very rarely feel in danger on my bike. An unacceptably high number of cyclists die on the roads each year, but it shouldn't put us off getting on our bikes. The more cyclists there are on the roads, the more other drivers know how to behave when they're around cyclists, how much space to give them, how to spot them, and how not to knock them off their bikes. But I still prefer to do my cycle to work without clipping into the pedals. After that first session in Finsbury Park, I went home, took off the cycle shoes, and put them away in the cupboard for another six months until a few days before my first ever triathlon.

KATIE

Wheeling and dealing:
Getting a bike for your first triathlon

Contrary to popular belief, you don't need to spend a fortune on a bike to start out in triathlon. If a 'Boris' bike can be ridden up the iconic climb, Mont Ventoux, in the French Alps, or even around the London Triathlon, then the chances are you can lay your hands on something that will get you through a sprint triathlon. At some of the more beginner-friendly races, you can expect to see a variety of bikes; in fact, the first time I completed Blenheim Triathlon, I remember overtaking a man in a polar bear costume pushing a bike with a basket up the hill.

There are many different types of bikes and, while you'll most commonly see road bikes at triathlons (or a version of them, called 'time trial' (TT) or 'triathlon' bikes), you could complete a shorter race on a mountain bike, or hybrid, without needing anything too specialist. If you don't own a bike, this should open up a few options for borrowing one from a friend. Having said that, the rules of triathlon (and common sense) state that your bike must be safe and roadworthy to take part in a triathlon. Bike helmets are also compulsory at all triathlons (and you'll be grateful for it when a polar bear approaches you at speed on his shopper).

Are you sitting comfortably?

Road bikes and triathlon bikes are used in triathlon because their handlebar set-up and narrow tyres mean that they can, potentially, go faster than something more 'comfortable'. They also look fast, which is just as important for many people. There is generally an inverse correlation between comfort and speed, so decide which of these is your priority. For a first triathlon, a comfortable ride might mean you're more likely to enjoy your race, and more likely to do another.

Of course, a bike needn't actually be uncomfortable. A bike may feel uncomfortable because you're not used to riding it or because it isn't set up right for you. In the same way that running hurts if you are not trained in it but also if you're attempting it in high heels a size too small. Comfort in cycling is primarily about getting the contact points in the right place between the rider and bike. A saddle that suits you, positioned in the right place, and at the right height, will also help; so too will doing some training and getting your bottom 'conditioned' for cycling. The position of your handlebars and the size of the bike frame are two other crucial features that will affect the comfort of all contact points between you and your bike. There are some rules of thumb to help with this fitting process, for example, your saddle should be at a height where, when the pedal is at the bottom, your legs should be very slightly bent with the ball of your foot on the pedal; if your hips rock from side to side when you pedal, this is a sure sign that your saddle needs to be moved down a bit. There are bike fitting services available at some specialist cycle retailers, which will work out exactly the right position for you on the bike; the free alternative is to ask a more experienced cyclist friend or cycling club members for advice when buying and setting up your bike. In the chapter Chamois, shorts and shelter, we'll discuss the importance of the padding in cycling shorts and tri suits and how they help with one crucial contact point between the rider and their bike.

How to make any bike go faster

Entire books have been written on this topic and are lapped up by cyclists and triathletes alike. Cycling enthusiasts can spend a fortune on modifying their bikes, and replacing components with lighter, shinier and allegedly more-fast-making bits. The first thing any bike aficionado will do when assessing a bicycle is to pick it up; however, weight is not the primary concern for going fast.

I'm going to let you into a secret that will make you faster for a fraction of the cost. You won't even have to do any extra training. Are you ready for this?

For most people, the simplest and cheapest way to go faster on a bike is to pump up your tyres.

True fact: at any one time, across the globe, the majority of bikes have too little air in their tyres. Don't let yours be one of them. Buying a good pump is a great investment in your triathlon future and it needn't cost you very much.

The next thing to look at is what cycle geeks call the 'transmission' (translation: chain and gears). Look carefully at your bike and ask yourself this: 'Is my chain brown?'

If the answer is 'Yes', this is not helping you. Likewise, you could ask yourself, 'When I change gear, does it sound like a spoon going down a waste-disposal unit?' Again, a positive response is not a good thing here. Wetsuits are not the only place where you'll need lubricant as a triathlete. When you're out buying your new pump, treat yourself to a bottle of chain oil.

It's worth saying now that if your chain is already brown, it probably needs replacing so take your bike along to a bike shop for a check-up by a professional. At the same time, ask them to take a look at your brakes. Counter-intuitively, these things that are designed to slow you down, are important for going fast. Good brakes will give you the confidence to go at your top speed and allow you to maximise the time you spend there.

What do I get for my money?

The cycling industry is booming in the UK so bike prices are becoming very competitive. Many manufacturers are recognising that more people are coming into cycling and triathlon looking for a good deal on an entry-level bike and there is now a good choice of quality road bikes starting at around £500. If you've decided to treat yourself to a road bike then start by deciding your budget and stick to it. It can be very tempting to get drawn into spending more once you've seen the shiny machines on offer in your local bike shop.

If £500 sounds a bit steep then new road bikes can be purchased for as little as £250 but there will be some compromise involved. Bear in mind that a price tag under £250 will get you a BSO (bike-shaped object) rather than a quality road bike, so if your budget is tight then buying second-hand may be a better option.

There is a huge range of road bikes on the market so do some research into what you can realistically get for your budget. Some of the main differences are:

Frame material: the frame is the big bit of the bike to which all other bits are attached. The most common material used in an entry-level bike frame tends to be aluminium as it is light and relatively inexpensive, compared to other materials, such as titanium or carbon fibre.

The 'bits': the moving parts of your bike (the chainset, derailleurs, gear shifters and brakeset) make up what's known as the 'groupset' and this can make up a surprising chunk of the bike cost. More expensive bikes tend have better quality groupsets fitted, and this is part of the reason that costs can quickly escalate.

The wheels: the round bits of your bike. An entry-level bike will come with a standard set of wheels that are perfectly serviceable. Since they are easy to take off and put back on, wheels are also a convenient way of upgrading part of your bike, if you wish to, at a later date.

'One careful owner'

Buying second-hand can get you 'more bike' for your money, particularly if you want above-basic specifications at an affordable price and don't mind not having the very latest versions or colours.

Sadly, there are lots of stolen bikes out there so don't be tempted to buy from the man in the pub. Online auction sites have proven to be a hot bed for off-loading stolen goods, so be cautious and check out the seller (e.g. feedback, previously sold items). A genuine seller should be happy to let you see the bike so always have a close inspection before you commit to buying – photos don't show squeaks and seized parts.

Internet forums can be a good place to buy from a genuine enthusiast without a middleman taking a cut. Buying from someone in your local cycling club or triathlon club is even better since you can get the claims of 'never crashed!' and 'never ridden in the rain!' independently verified with eye witness statements.

By far the best way to buy a second-hand bike is to get to know a cycling enthusiast who has 1) more money than sense, and 2) an acute need to always have the very newest and shiniest cycling paraphernalia. The recent boom in cycling and triathlon appears to be producing more of these types of people. You can offer them a useful service of taking their barely used, now-not-quite-the-latest bike off their hands, enabling them to free up space in their garage and minimise the suspicions of their partner regarding their ever-expanding bicycle portfolio.

Let's talk shop

Online bike retailers can offer great prices on new bikes but they do lack the personal touch. You may need some mechanical confidence to make a successful Internet bike purchase; especially if you end up inadvertently buying a box of bits that still needs assembling. Getting the right size based on a few photos and dimensions can be difficult too; so visiting a cycle store is really the better option for buying your first road bike.

Cycle retailers fall into three main categories:

The cycle supermarket offers competitive prices but often a limited selection and an absence of 'high-end' brands. The cycle connoisseur would never be openly seen entering a cycle supermarket, although they may pop in under a disguise to avoid paying £10 for some oil for their chain. As they work in big volumes, some of the better retailers in this bracket are able to offer some excellent deals on entry-level road bikes, and some of their newer brands reaching that market are designed to meet the needs of performance cyclists while offering great value for money. Unfortunately, with some of these retailers, you may not experience the personal retail service or expertise of a more specialist bike shop: I was once offered an insurance policy in case I ever found myself with a 'buckled tyre' (for the record, tyres do not tend to buckle; it is the rim of the wheel that succumbs to such misshaping). If you are offered a policy like this, it should not inspire much confidence in the mechanical aptitude of your service provider.

The traditional cycle shop has seen its business squeezed by online retailers, and from both bottom and top by the new cycle supermarkets and boutiques, respectively. To counter these threats, the cycle shop has redoubled its traditional approaches to sales. The main tactic is to cram the shop with a dazzling selection of bicycles, components and accessories. So, unless you are already a cycling expert, you will need the assistance of a competent salesperson to guide you through the baffling choices on offer. Don't be afraid to ask for help: traditional cycle shops are typically staffed by cycling enthusiasts with lots of expertise.

The cycle boutique is a fairly recent phenomenon that has developed primarily to harness those prepared to spend lots of money on a bike. In contrast to the traditional cycle shop, the cycle boutique is not a shop, it is more of a concept. It is not crammed with bicycles. Instead, you will find minimal stock, strategically placed under enhanced lighting, giving an appearance more reminiscent of an art gallery than a cycle retailer. Expect an enthusiastic, lavish and 'bespoke' service once engaged with a cycle boutique salesperson but don't expect to leave without threatening your credit card limit on essentials such as cycling shoes crafted from yak leather.

What next?

With two wheels and a bike helmet, you're now equipped to take on a triathlon, but if your new road bike and first triathlon have inspired you to do more, then there are a couple of optional extras that tend to come next:

Cycling shoes and clip-in pedals: cycle-specific shoes that fix to a specialist pedal take a bit of practice clipping in and out but it's worth the effort. The reason they are so popular is because they allow more efficient transfer of force from your legs to the bike. Imagine trying to put a nail into a wall with a leg of ham, and then try using a hammer.

'Time trial' (TT) bars: these are extensions that clip to your road bike handlebars and, in theory, allow you to tuck your body into a more aerodynamic position as you ride. Before you go out and purchase a pair to attach to your bike, bear in mind that poorly positioned TT bars can be less use than no TT bars at all. 'Time trial' bikes are fitted with integrated bars, where the extension and handlebars come as one piece and the gear shifters fit into the ends of the extensions; this is one of the main differences between a road bike and a time trial bike. Getting the position right and, most importantly, practising riding in this position are crucial if they are going to make you any quicker: after all, you can only go faster if you remain on your bike.

Of course, now that you've bought your first road bike, kitted yourself out with new shoes, and started looking at time trial bikes, you may find yourself at the top of a slippery slope leading towards multiple bike purchases. A winter training bike, a summer training bike, a race bike, a commuting bike and a pub bike can each justifiably service a niche requirement that just one bike would never do. This is why cyclists and triathletes often refer to the following mathematical rule:

Ideal number of bikes to own = n + 1, where n is the number of bikes you currently own.

An alternative but lesser known rule, yet one that's also worth bearing in mind, is this:

Ideal number of bikes to own = x − 1, where x is the number of bikes it would take for your partner to move out.

It's just one of the many reasons why I'm so grateful that I live with a cyclist.

KATIE

To an injury and beyond: Becoming a runner

'Imagine what you could do if you did some training,' said Laura with a grin on her face, a medal around her neck and a glass of prosecco in her hand.

We'd just finished the Frankfurt marathon when she planted that seed in my head. Perhaps by this point you might be curious to know how Laura and I became friends. We grew up on opposite sides of the country, we do different jobs and we live in different cities. We might have easily gone through life never bumping into one another. Yet we managed to become friends over two years before we actually met in person. As Laura says, 'Not long ago the question "How did you two meet?" would have been met with embarrassed looks and mumbles if the honest response was "we met online".'

We tend to imagine that the Internet is full of predators, trolls and perverts lurking indecently behind their keyboards. Yet the Internet can be a powerful way to connect people with common interests, and Laura is one of the amazing people I have met 'online' by writing about something we are both completely passionate about: running.

Completing a triathlon requires the ability to cover the distance in each sport; going fast in triathlon requires strength in all three. While my swimming is acceptable and, given the right course, my cycling isn't far behind, my run in any triathlon is a textbook demonstration of being constantly overtaken. Being passionate about running doesn't have to mean that I'm any good at it. Laura, on the other hand, has become an accomplished runner, with an enviable marathon PB and a coaching qualification. For the sake of your triathlon future, we thought you might appreciate it if we swap roles for now and let Laura give out the advice in the next chapter. Instead, I'll tell you how I became a runner.

On 1 January 1984, my dad organised Hereford's first New Year's Day 10 k. He tells me great stories of the first couple of runs: people still tiddly from the night before having to call the 'big white telephone' before the start, and a team from the local hostelry pushing a full barrel of cider around the course for charity. The event became more and more popular and he handed over the organisation to a local running club in the early 1990s. Too small to run (my brothers did, but it appears the line was drawn at 11 years old in the 1980s), I think I might have spent nine New Year's Day mornings perfecting the art of fastening safety pins into groups of four and handing them to the runners with a grin. I often now wonder why there aren't more infants enlisted to help with this task at races. Every year, I would ask my dad, 'What's that smell?'

'Embrocation,' came his reply each time.

It's why I still think that 'embrocation' is a word used to describe the combined stench of muscle rub, coffee, cider, B.O., fart and dread. The event is still going more than 30 years later. I'm old enough to run it now and my brothers and I can usually be found trading excuses at the start line on 1 January.

Running was a big part of family life, whether it was helping at Dad's events or running a 5 k with my mum; there are a lot of memories tied up with that smell of embrocation. Participation wasn't always voluntary though, and, at school, I was simply the one silly enough to say 'Yes' when no one else was prepared to finish last in the 1,500 m against the fast girls. After school, I kept up a sideline interest in running as a way to keep fit for other sports but I still wouldn't have called myself a 'runner'. That came much later.

I've heard it said that you should run your first marathon for the right reasons and that the 'right' reasons shouldn't be because your spouse, boss or neighbour two doors down once did it. I'm not sure where 'entering a marathon because your squiffy mate, Chrissy, said she was going to and you were so squiffy you agreed' stands as a reason but that's how I found myself entering my first marathon in 2005. The truth is, I'd always wanted to be able to say I'd done a marathon. My dad ran one when I was very small (apparently I spectated from my pushchair asking helpfully, 'Where's Daddy? Why is he taking so long? Why does he look like that?'), and I'd been entering the London Marathon ballot in a very non-committal way, and accumulating a small stack of rejection memorabilia, for a couple of years running up to this. It wasn't long before Chrissy's persuasive nature had taken further victims and a crew of five were preparing to tackle our maiden marathon. 'How had she managed to do this?' you might ask. By disguising this test of endurance as a jolly weekend jaunt to Amsterdam is how.

I don't remember exactly what I did in terms of trying to find a training programme but I do know that I can't have followed it very well. I do seem to remember thinking I was still quite fit from rowing and cycling (this was a delusion); I also sprained my ankle playing netball about five months before the marathon, thus enabling me to procrastinate a little further before starting with the training (this was unwise); finally, I remember going out for one long run, where I ran as far as I could, basing my mileage on an approximation of 10 minutes/mile and came home when I was tired after 3 hours or so, claiming it to have been at least 18 miles (this was totally inaccurate and wildly short of the mark, I later discovered using Google Maps).

So, in hindsight, my training had been delusional, unwise and inaccurate (I don't think I'm spoiling anything to tell you now that Laura's advice won't be based on a plan like this). It was lucky then that I was blissfully unaware of this. In fact, the scale of the task we had undertaken only really began to hit home while perusing a map of the course over a pizza the night before. Fortunately, we had unwittingly installed ourselves on a table outside the pizzeria, directly opposite one of Amsterdam's coffee houses, and we grew passively more positive as the evening wore on.

Race morning arrived and we faced the first task of finding some breakfast before locating the right train to take us to the out of town start. Chrissy was on the ball and got us to the right platform, but we were less prepared with the nutritional aspects and grabbed ourselves some coffee and croissants from a grubby kiosk at the station. The journey was a truly enlightening experience: firstly, by meeting a chap we called '100 Marathon Man'; he had a special T-shirt on proclaiming this and he took great pride in warning us that we were grossly unprepared for the day's events. Secondly, we discovered that the train journey was just long enough to take our intestines through to the final phases of caffeine's effects. We hurriedly bid farewell to our new friend and trotted as fast as we could to the Portaloos and start line.

As for the run itself, I think I remember four main aspects of the course:

1. Three laps of a stadium – one at the start, one halfway through and one at the finish. The one halfway forced me to go to my special place and have a stern chat with myself;

2. A 5 mile stretch out and back along a river – here, I saw thousands of runners on the other side of the river at least 10 miles ahead of me. I visited my special place again;

3. An industrial estate: the part of the course where tumbleweed replaced spectators;

4. The finish: specifically, having to do a final lap of that track, the kind lady who took my timing tag off because I couldn't bend down, and eventually finding my cheering friends who had all finished before me.

I have few other memories of the run itself, except that I know I have rarely been more relieved to finish a race. And that I wore more sports drink than I drank after several hours of sloshing it over myself from crumpled plastic cups. Perhaps I sound a little negative about my first marathon, but I was pretty gutted at this point. Gutted at myself for preparing so badly and gutted to find out that I wasn't as fit as I thought. Maybe I did enter for the wrong reasons.

Following Amsterdam, I was certain that I had to run another marathon and, more importantly, that it had to be better than the first experience. My friends were reassuringly keen for another adventure too, so we settled on a weekend away to run Dublin Marathon, a year later. Luckily, my failings at Amsterdam were solely due to my own inadequacies, so that was fairly easy to remedy; I consulted the *Runner's World* 'ultimate' training schedules and decided to put in the advised 16 weeks of hard work, instead of the ten weeks of faffing and denial I'd resorted to previously. I also bought a GPS watch that would stop me lying to myself about the distance of my 'long' runs.

In Amsterdam, we learned a lot about appropriate preparation on the day of the marathon. In Dublin, we learned exactly what to do the day before: namely, a trip to the Guinness factory for my first ever pint of this nutritious, yet delicious, sports drink. We were even organised enough to sort out some breakfast for the race morning and looked very wise and experienced as we ate our muesli and yogurt, instead of the sad pastries and cold coffee, at 6 a.m. in our youth hostel common room. We even took pity on a nice Swedish man who was eating just a very brown banana for sustenance. We saw him later that day and found out he'd run the race in about two and a half hours, we liked to think it was partly thanks to our mercy muesli.

The start in the centre of the city was a big improvement on the train journey to the outskirts of Amsterdam, but the crowded streets made it slow going to the start line; still, chip timing saved any worries and it wasn't long before we were on our way in what remains one of my favourite marathons to date. There was support throughout the course: from shouts of encouragement to hand-outs of sweets and lollies. Local children had devised dance routines to keep the runners going and families had set up makeshift water tables outside their houses. The training had also paid off, meaning I could enjoy the distractions while I kept moving. I finished in 4 hours 7 minutes, a 40 minute improvement on my Amsterdam time, and in the finishers' photo I had a bigger smile than the one taken twelve months previously. You'd be right to wonder how the weekend could have got much better, but it did: James Brown had taken his 'Seven Decades of Funk World Tour' to Dublin that weekend and, passing the theatre, we managed to score some last minute tickets to watch his gig that night. The bouncer was very apologetic that our seats at the front on the balcony were 'too dangerous' for us to stand up and dance on; we grinned and accepted his apology, happy to rest our weary legs and let the now late, great Mr Brown do the moving.

Shortly after Dublin, I hit a bit of a tricky patch at work, so I threw myself wholeheartedly into the running to take my mind off it. The GPS watch wasn't just useful for tracking distance, but I could see my times for each run, and push myself to get faster. By the following spring, I'd trimmed a good chunk off my 10 k and half marathon times, and was looking forward to my first triathlons since discovering that sports bras could be employed. Keen to test myself at a marathon again, I set my sights on the Berlin Marathon and the target of a 'Good for Age' time to finally secure that elusive London Marathon entry. I downloaded the next training programme and found myself running five or six days a week in preparation.

'You were my tailwind and are all record breaking runners too!' said Haile Gebrselassie after he set a new world record at the Berlin Marathon in 2007.

I shared the road with this great man that day but it wasn't the tailwind I could feel while waiting in the start pen. Packed into the crowd, I noticed a warm sensation spreading down the back of my legs. Was it the collective tingle of nervous anticipation? No. It was the tepid sprinkle of a man's urination. On foreign soil and not knowing enough German to scold the perpetrator, I used my best international frown and shrug to ask him what he thought he was up to. He looked me in the eye and said in a London accent, 'What's your problem? You'll have a shower at the end.'

It wasn't an ideal start but at least it took my mind off the nerves from the pressure I was feeling about the pace I had to run. There was also a niggling feeling in my knee that I'd been trying to ignore for the last three weeks before the race, and I welcomed any distraction from that, even if the distraction was disgusting. The first 10 miles went by on track and without event, and I was looking forward to seeing some friends supporting me at the next mile marker. Unfortunately, the niggle was still there, and had been lurking menacingly for the past hour or so. No one likes to be ignored, and neither do knee pains; at 10 miles, my knee buckled underneath me and that niggle played out a tantrum to rival a hungry toddler. I stretched, grimaced and pushed on, just far enough to get past my friends. Then it buckled again. And it kept doing so every time I got back up to pace. I could manage a walk or a slow jog but nothing more, and I kept that up for the next 16 miles to finish one minute faster than I did in Dublin the year before, and 25 minutes outside my target time. I'd trained so hard for that race that a one minute PB did little to console me. It turns out that I trained too hard, which is too often a lesson learned the difficult way in running. Still, I would think back to the man in the start pen: my race didn't go to plan that day but, in dark times, there are rare occasions when it's OK to hope that someone has a worse race than you.

The knee injury persisted for a few months after Berlin; long enough for me to get completely out of the habit of running, and long enough to have decided on a career change that made sense professionally, but pushed the work-life balance back firmly into the hands of work. It was as if all the best excuses had aligned like planets in the universe of exercise-induced apathy.

When I started running again, I was frustrated by all the fitness I'd lost and struggled to find the motivation to get out and go training. I kept entering races but wasn't enjoying what I was doing. It wasn't a feature I admired in myself. I'd worked really hard to become a 'runner' and it was something I wanted to be again. So, I started writing a blog to give my withering self-motivation a kick up the bum and train for another marathon. After a couple of failed attempts to get marathon fit, I finally got that London ballot entry; I had a reason to train and there was something to write about. I didn't really tell any friends or family about the blog at first, but it gained a small following of other running bloggers and one of them was Laura, who cheered from the virtual sidelines to the finish line of the London Marathon.

Something I began to realise that I'd forgotten was how running gives me the space to think; something I struggle to find in a normal day. I think it's all the jiggling up and down that somehow seems to help the little worries filter down, leaving room for ideas and answers to drop in uninvited. Not that I ever resolve any of the big stuff while I'm out running. You only have to google 'Bill Clinton in short running shorts' to realise why it would never be a good idea to try and solve life's bigger problems during a run. Writing about running works well with the way my brain reacts to a good run around. Instead of obsessing over the numbers on my GPS, as I used to, I try to think of the story I could tell. It forces me to focus on the good bits, or if there are no good bits, then at least the funny bits. It has become a bit of a mantra that there are no such things as bad races, just good stories. Writing about running means that Berlin is no longer the marathon where I got injured, but the marathon where a man peed on my leg in the start pen. I think of myself as a 'runner' again now, not because I'm fast, or lean, or look good in a pair of Clinton-esque short shorts, but because I have learned to love it again.

Above all, writing about running has allowed me to meet more friends like Chrissy and our merry band of Amsterdam marathoners. Friends like Laura, who take as little convincing as I do to enter a race, book an air fare, and try to cram enough energy gels into the hand luggage liquid allowance. As she says, 'The greatest thing the Internet can do for us is bring us together. To connect us with other people, to share knowledge and experience. And though the connections we make through it and the friendships we form are no less valid because they haven't been made in person – when they are taken offline and into the real world it's pretty awesome.'

In October 2013, we took a trip to the Frankfurt Marathon with two other friends. My preparation had been a bit relaxed, which had become a bit of an ongoing joke with Laura and the others. The way I see it, I run far less than I used to but I run more than I did when I was injured; this might mean that I turn up to races a bit undertrained, but I'd always rather that than a miserable morning like the one I had in Berlin. It's also the only way I'll fit in the other sports I love: cycling and swimming. I was thrilled to finish in 4.5 hours, which is what prompted Laura's provocation over the glass of bubbly. Perhaps it sounded a bit harsh but I know Laura and I know she had a good point: I started marathon running for the challenge, so turning up underprepared wasn't necessarily fulfilling that. Instead, Laura's comment helped me to decide, after years of thinking about it, to join a running club, which would help with the motivation to keep running over the winter, and introduce me to more amazing people who love the sport. It also helped me to reach a decision when I was going back and forth over whether to do another iron-distance triathlon. And it dared me to enter a new race with a challenging circuit that would push me even more than the Midnight Man had.

LAURA

One foot in front of the other: How to get up and running

Running is by far the simplest (by which I mean, the least technical) of the three triathlon disciplines. This is not to say it's any easier than the other two. You do, however, need less stuff and can do it pretty much wherever and whenever you want. Any idiot can run: it's just a case of putting one foot in front of the other in quick succession. Run like an idiot, however, and before too long you might find yourself getting injured.

I ran like an idiot when I first started. My plan, when I first stepped onto a treadmill seven years ago, was to see how long I could run for and then, the next time, try to run further than that. And repeat, and repeat. It's not surprising that I got injured. My first mistake was stepping onto a treadmill instead of running outside. The treadmill offered a security blanket for me, but it was also painfully dull and uninspiring. Sometimes running outside is a bit hot, a bit cold, a bit wet and a bit too open to being spotted by people you know. But once you get going and decide to accept all those issues, it really is so much nicer than trudging along like a hamster on a wheel, brushing elbows with someone who is looking at the numbers on your treadmill and pushing theirs up a notch.

Starting from scratch

I teach non-runners how to run. Every ten weeks I have a new group of women, many of whom haven't run since school. They arrive on the first week, nervous that they'll be the slowest, that they won't be able to keep up and that they won't be able to do it. I've taught women of all shapes and sizes, from their 20s to their 60s, and helped them go on to complete a 5 k. Age and size are no barriers to being able to run 5 k; all it requires is patience and perseverance.

Start small and build up gradually

In week one, we run for one minute at a time. This sounds simple, but many of my runners quickly come to realise how long a minute can feel. It isn't the sexy or glamorous notion of running that many of us have – we usually picture ourselves gliding effortlessly through open countryside, churning out laps of the park and returning home glowing and smiling. Running is rarely like that. Running for a minute and then stopping to walk can feel dispiriting. It can make you feel embarrassed as other runners whizz past you. But most runners can remember what it feels like to be in this position, and if you stick with it and gradually do more running and less walking, you'll find it more effective and more enjoyable than running to your limit and then collapsing in a heap.

Faster, stronger, longer

There are two main things runners of all abilities are looking to do: run faster or run further. Some want to do both. The advice is simple: if you want to run further, run slower; if you want to run faster, run faster. Training for my first ultramarathon was a daunting prospect as I looked at all those miles on my plan; that was until I realised I could run them as slow as I liked. It took a few runs to get out of the habit of falling into my marathon pace, but once I left my ego at home, I found I liked running slowly. This also came in handy for the iron-distance marathon run.

Running faster should come in the form of some structured speed sessions; either intervals or tempo runs. Intervals, often done on a track but easy to do anywhere that you've got a flat bit of ground, free from obstacles, are usually done just once a week. The interval of running is commonly anything from 400 m to 1 mile. You run it faster than your easy pace, you have a set recovery jog, and then you run it 2–11 more times depending on your fitness and the length of your interval. Tempo runs are a longer stretch of running (anything from 1 to 8 miles) done at a 'comfortably hard' pace. You shouldn't be able to hold a conversation easily while you're doing a tempo run.

Speed work can be difficult to do by yourself. They're not the most tempting of runs to get you out the door, so I recommend doing them with a friend. Which brings me neatly on to the next point.

Join a group or club

Katie has already suggested you join a triathlon club. If you've got room in your wallet for another card, there's no reason you can't also join a running club; Katie is a member of one of each. I'm a member of the Serpentine Running Club, which also has a triathlon division, though I've never trained with them other than the odd spin session. What they also have, and something I've taken full advantage of, is lots of knowledgeable coaches and plenty of coached speed and hill sessions. It's much easier to talk yourself into a track session where there's going to be 50 friendly faces waiting for you and some the same speed as you to try and keep up with. If you want to run longer or run faster, run with people who can do just that and are happy to show you how. A good coach will be able to look at how you run and give you a few simple pointers to help your running form that would help you more than dedicating this whole chapter to the subject ever could.

Running clubs, like the runners they serve, come in all shapes and sizes. Serpentine has more than 2,000 members, but many will have a fraction of that. If you're thinking of joining one, get in touch with them and go down to a session or two to see if you like the feel of it before joining up. The UK Athletics website (www.britishathletics.org.uk) has a club search option, as do the governing bodies of the sport in the individual nations.

Kit

Like most aspects of triathlon, there really is no limit to the amount of money it's possible to spend on running kit. But the bits you ultimately need, can be found quite cheaply. You'll need a pair of running shoes and some of you might need a sports bra, and that's essentially it. For your first few runs, just wear whatever you're comfortable in – an old T-shirt and a pair of leggings will get you round a mile or two. As you run more and increase your distance, you can experiment and find what you feel happier in. Those big running questions like capri tights or shorts? Short sleeves or a vest? This brand or that? It all comes down to personal preference. If you're running when it's dark out though, get yourself some high-visibility items. You can pick up a bright yellow vest for a couple of quid and however unflattering it might look, it's a much better look than being run over.

Deep breath, and relax

One question my beginners ask a lot is 'How do I breathe?' I always respond with 'How are you breathing now?' We don't think about breathing in our day-to-day life, it happens unconsciously, and I'm a firm believer that you should let your body keep control of this area while running too. I've heard various advice about breathing in for a number of counts and then out for a number, but I've always found it too complicated. Your mouth is the biggest opening leading to your lungs, so it makes sense to use this over your nose to maximise the amount of air going in and out. Other than that, trust your body on this one, it knows what it's doing.

Tri run distances

If you're coming to triathlon from a running background, you'll be familiar with the length of the run section of the standard triathlon distances: 5 km, 10 km and 13.1 and 26.2 miles. They're taken from common running race lengths. If you're a non-runner looking to get into triathlon, you'll be able to find plenty of running events that match the distance you'll need to run and plenty of training plans to guide you as to how to build up to the various distances. Running in a triathlon, however, is like no other running you'll do. After all that swimming and cycling, your legs are going to complain when you first ask them to run. Practising cycling and then running straight after it has more benefit than giving you two workouts for the price of one and a pile of smelly kit – it's a genuine bona fide technique to make you get better at, well, cycling and then running, just as you need to do in a triathlon (see Takeaway training advice).

Learn to enjoy it

For the last 10 miles of the bike leg of my first half iron-distance triathlon, I cried. Not just tears but big fat sobs. Afterwards, I thought a lot about why I'd cried like that. I was exhausted, but I wasn't in pain. Partly the tears were fear – I was scared that the run was going to be uncomfortable and that I was going to hate it. A half marathon seemed like a long way to run after all that swimming and cycling.

As I prepared for my iron-distance triathlon, I knew that for the last 12 miles of the cycle I'd be thinking about the run I'd have to do once I stopped pedalling. There'd be 26.2 miles to run before the finish. Having good marathon experiences in the memory bank was important for me to avoid crying my way through 112 miles of cycling.

When Katie and I travelled to the Frankfurt Marathon with a couple of friends, I'd agreed to pace our friend Liz to a 4-hour marathon. Good experiences don't come much better than trotting 26.2 miles with a friend, photobombing a few race pictures, and finishing with a smile at a German disco party. And that was what I hoped I would try to think about as I cycled round the ironman.

If you're preparing for your first sprint, get out and run a 5 km at a comfortable pace. Take a friend with you, don't look at your watch and plan to finish somewhere you can go for a coffee and a cake. Go somewhere nice, run the distance you'll need to do at the end of your triathlon and bank your own good experiences. Then when race day comes and you're hurtling along on your bike preparing to dismount, you'll be excited, not intimidated by the idea of putting on your running shoes. Learn to love running and you'll look forward to it.

LAURA

Somebody has to come last:
Becoming a triathlete

To: 'Katie King'
Subject: Tricurious

I was about to enter: 'How do I train for one of these triathlon things?' into Google but thought I'd ask you instead.

Here's my plan so far...

November - No running. Some swimming. Fall off new bike.
December - Some running. Some swimming. Learn how not to fall off new bike.
January - Start marathon training. Forget about swimming and cycling.
February - Injure myself running. Get back on bike.

March - Oh my lordy, I have a marathon next month!
April - Run marathon. Oh my lordy, I have a triathlon next month!
May - Drown in river.

To: 'Laura Fountain'
Subject: RE: Tricurious

Tricurious? That would be a good title for a book.
I like your plan. (Except the drowning bit. No need for that.)

It's 5.30 a.m. on a Sunday morning. I've got a number scrawled on my hand and a bad feeling in my stomach. It's just like the good old clubbing days, except I'm getting up instead of going to bed, and the number written on my hand is only three digits long: 282 – my race number for my first ever triathlon.

In the theatre world they have a saying: 'Bad dress rehearsal, good opening night'. For a while, I'd taken solace in this saying, reassuring myself that my triathlon 'opening night' would go without a hitch. But there'd been no dress rehearsal: I'd broken all the rules about trying all your kit out before race day and didn't even take the price tag off my all-in-one triathlon suit until the morning of the race. I'd dragged my wetsuited self into a lake twice. While it quelled my fears about sinking to the bottom of the river without a trace on race day, it hardly filled me with confidence. In the week leading up to the event, I swam in a pool for 750 metres, non-stop – the same distance as a sprint distance triathlon. My lane at the pool was occupied by me and one other swimmer and, quite frankly, that was one too many for my liking. I'd heard the horror stories of people getting punched and kicked in triathlon swim starts, of goggles flying off and swimmers being pushed under, and I was terrified it was going to happen to me.

My first race was in St Neots in Cambridgeshire: the Nice Tri Sprint Triathlon. It's half an hour from where I grew up in Peterborough and my friend, Helen, lives less than a mile from the start. When I phoned her up to ask if I could come and stay the night before the race, she was welcoming. 'So you're going to swim in the river? The one in town?' she said.

'Yes.'

'But won't it be really cold?'

'Probably.'

'Well, good luck mate but rather you than me.'

I'd arrived on the train from London with all my kit crammed into a backpack, and cycled the 2 miles to Helen's house. She made me dinner and asked me what time I'd be getting up.

'Well the race starts at eight a.m. ish so... '

'Eight a.m.? You're joking! Why does it have to be so early?'

It was a shock to me too. I was used to doing running events that start somewhere between 9 a.m. and 11 a.m. Triathletes, I was starting to realise, like to get things going early.

• • •

The next morning, I lowered myself into the Great Ouse river. My hands were cold but the rest of my body was warm enough. The water was 12°C, another important number. Half a degree lower and our swim would have been shortened to 400 m. I wasn't sure which situation I would have preferred.

A horn sounded and my wave of 57 women started swimming. Elbows and feet flailed around in all directions – this is what I'd worried most about. I hadn't worried about my own swimming. I knew I could slowly complete the course by myself without getting into difficulty, but I worried about the other swimmers. That someone else would panic and grab hold of me. That an elbow to the face would knock off my goggles and make me panic too. That a kick to the chest could leave me winded and unable to swim. Fear can be a good thing. It can give you the extra adrenaline you need on race day. But as the race got underway, it was my biggest threat. The anxiousness that I felt made my chest tighten and my breathing hurried – two things that aren't useful at any time, let alone when you're trying to swim in a straight line and not take a lungful of water.

I let the pack head off before I started to swim and I stayed close to the bank. Too close. After about 50 metres, I got weeds in my mouth. This threw me. This doesn't happen down Kentish Town pool. I pulled them out and tried to carry on swimming but my stroke was all wonky and wrong. My mum, my dad and Helen were walking along the bank next to me, cheering me on. I thought how concerned they must be that it didn't look like it was going terribly well. My dad would be considering taking off his shoes and rolling up his trouser legs, ready to leap in and save me. I was still too close to the bank and my hands were getting caught in the weeds as I tried to pull through the water, but I was worried about going deeper. Soon I would have no choice. The turnaround buoy appeared faster than it should have, thanks to the outward swim being with the flow of the river. I crossed over and hoped. In the deeper water, my stroke got better. I was swimming slightly lopsided due to only breathing on one side, but it looked more like swimming than splashing. My confidence grew and I even passed another swimmer. As I passed another woman doing breaststroke, she called out to her supporters on the river bank, 'I can't put my face in, it's too cold.'

One of the canoe club members, who were patrolling the swim, pulled another swimmer out of the water, but I carried on.

Despite almost swimming into a boat moored at the side, the upstream swim went better. If I'd managed to swim in a straight line, I might even have looked like I knew what I was doing. I approached the last buoy and swam headfirst into a man from the wave ahead. Steering myself was still proving a problem. 'Sorry – my fault,' I said, and then immediately did it again.

Another 10 metres and it was over. Two pairs of hands helped pull me up the bank and I lunged towards transition. The transition area was empty and I was a bit delirious from the swim as I staggered towards my metre-wide allocation of space – a combination of the cold, the exhaustion and the delight at having survived. I pulled off my wetsuit in a PB time, put my bike kit on, and headed towards the bike course.

Helen had driven me around the 14-mile bike loop the day before, which had helped me familiarise myself with where I had to turn left. This was lucky because, by the time I got on my bike, there was nobody around to follow. After a mile, the guy I'd just swum into came zooming past me on his bike, managing to do so without colliding with me. I was eating a Snickers bar at the time. I pedalled fast but with nobody around to get competitive with I had to just do my own thing and try to keep the tempo up. My legs moaned but the countryside roads were nice; I cycled past fields of oil seed rape, saw a hare hopping across the farmland, and a snowy owl circling overhead. It was a route that wanted me to slow down and enjoy it, not tear through it. With a third of the course to go, another woman overtook me. I tried to keep her in sight but she lost me on a couple of the small hills. Then, as we turned back towards the town, I saw another woman ahead of me and I made it my goal to overtake her before the bike section was complete. I passed her with a few hundred metres to go only for her to run off out of transition before me.

The run was the part of the race I was looking forward to and the bit that I could legitimately call a 'race'. It was two laps of a park by the river where we'd started and I would see my parents and Helen as I got off my bike and ran around. But it didn't go to plan. My feet were numb from getting cold in the river and not warming up on the bike, and every time I put a foot down it felt like my leg was going to keep going through the ground below it. As I ran out of transition, I could see a large group of people huddled round the finish area chatting: they'd already finished the race. There was a real chance I was going to come last. I overtook the woman I'd just passed on the bike and felt relieved that it might now be second from last. There were more people ahead of me but, as the run was a two-lap course, I couldn't tell if they were on their first or second lap. I ran past them all the same and pressed on, wanting it to be over. Breathing-wise I felt fine and I didn't get the lungs-in-mouth feeling that's usual on a 5 km, but my legs felt like lead. As I headed out for the second lap of the park, there was nobody left to pass. I counted down in my head to the finish and crossed the line.

I'd started the race with three goals: don't drown on the swim, don't fall off the bike, and complete the race. I hadn't had a time goal for the triathlon and I hadn't even worn a watch. I wanted to do the 5 km in under 25 minutes, and, as a rough estimate, I thought the bike would take around 1:10 but, as I hadn't ever cycled at top speed in preparation, only commuting to and from work, it was difficult to judge. I printed out my results at the finishing line and was very pleased with the numbers that popped up, total time: 1:54:52. Swim: 24:36, bike: 1:01:58, run: 22:58. As I staggered over the line, my first words to my supporters were: 'Never again.' But after I'd showered the river out of my hair and drunk a pint of beer, I knew that I'd started something that I had to see through to the end.

Just five weeks later, I was preparing to take on an 'Olympic' distance event at the Marlow Triathlon: a race twice as long as my first. But, this time, I had company, or at least until the race got underway. Katie was racing too and, although she was going to be much faster than me, it was nice to have someone to go through a few pre-race rituals with. We huddled on the bank of the Thames for the race briefing. 'Straight down the river and round this bend for seven hundred and fifty metres. Go round the fourth large buoy and then come back. We'll be here to help pull you out of the water.'

The race officials stood on the bank wearing jeans. 'They're going to get very wet and heavy by the time the day is over. He should have worn a nice pair of shorts,' I said to Katie.

'I wish they'd hurry up. I've been holding in a wee,' she replied.

The first two waves headed off round the bend of the river. 'Right then, there are only pink swim caps left,' said the race official, 'which can only mean one thing... '

'Gender stereotyping!' said Katie.

We climbed into the river, which was surprisingly warmer than I'd expected. I lowered my shoulders under the surface and pulled the neck of my wetsuit out to let the water in as my companion had instructed me to. It seemed a counter-intuitive way to get warm but I went along with it.

'Three, two, one... ' An air horn sounded and the mass of pink swim hats surged forward.

'I haven't finished my wee!'

We hung back for a moment, me to take up my rightful place at the back out of the way of elbows and faster swimmers and Katie to complete her pre-race ritual. Twenty-five minutes later, Katie climbed out of the water next to an official in sodden denim. She had swum her way through the pack and was the fifth woman to finish the swim leg. Meanwhile, I was taking things at a more pedestrian pace.

There are several benefits to being a slow triathlete. For starters, you don't have to worry about storming in and out of transition and getting on your bike the wrong way round. Taking your time to sit down, dry your feet and put your socks on (possibly even having a wee while you're sat on the grass) is unlikely to make any difference at all to your finish position. You get to talk to the cheery marshals and stewards too. This includes the one in a canoe who is your own personal chaperone as you're the 'last lady'. This is much like the position of First Lady, only better because you earned it entirely on your own.

I swam along the Thames in last place; careful to heed the advice my mum had emailed me the day before to 'stay out of the shallows'. My hand brushed something. Oh my God, was that a dead dog? Maybe it was worse, it could be a corpse. Don't think about it, just keep swimming. My swim was going better than last time – my zigzags were smaller and I managed to swim more front crawl and less breaststroke. But it was still slow.

'Nearly at the turn and then the river will take you back,' my chaperone informed me.

I put my face down and told myself, no more rests until the turn, and then, no more rests. Full stop. Before I knew it, 1,500 m had gushed by and I'd managed not to get elbowed or kicked by any other swimmers. I was hauled out of the water by two more marshals – no waiting in line for me like the speedsters at the other end of the race. I sat on the bank for a moment and had a little chat with them.

'How was that?'

'Not too bad in the second half, took me a while to get going though.'

'Want me to unzip your wetsuit?'

'Yes, please.' And with that, off I went. I got on my bike and started making my way through my picnic of six fig rolls, two Snickers bars, and a bottle of some sugary concoction. It was probably a little excessive but it kept me busy and distracted me for a couple of hours, if nothing else. I pedalled along with nobody around to hear me swearing loudly at 1) the wind in my face, 2) the potholed road, and 3) the hills. I got to around 6 miles and saw Katie speeding back towards transition in the other direction and calling out her encouragement: 'Go on, Laura!'

Another half hour passed, during which I busied myself playing a game called 'Where's the turnaround?' before I found the traffic cone and marshal signalling that I was half way through the triathlon. I thought about it as I cycled back towards the transition area and calculated that, if I wanted to do an ironman, I'd have to do three more triathlons: two half iron-distance races and then the big one. 'Just three more times,' I said to myself. Put like that it almost sounded doable. I was ignoring the fact that the races I'd have to do were much longer distances.

The return leg of the cycle followed the same route that I'd just ridden along. I passed a couple of people who were fixing punctures or dragging their broken bikes back towards the transition, but other than that there was no sign of cyclists. There was nobody behind me and I was still the last lady. Eventually, I climbed off my bike, ready to start the run, and I do like a nice run. It turns out that running after 1,500 m of swimming and 24 miles of cycling doesn't fall into the category of 'nice' as far as my legs were concerned. Like my first triathlon, the run was a two-lap course. The route followed the river along a trail and then turned off on more substantial paths to loop back to the start. As I approached the end of my first lap, a well-meaning steward called out to me: 'Nearly there. Just round this corner and you're finished.'

'I've got another lap.'

'Oh. Well keep going then.'

I passed the finishing line where Katie stood already holding her medal. She urged me on. On the second lap, I knew that each person I overtook meant another position between last place and me. The run was hard and I had to walk parts of the trail section along the Thames, but no matter how slow I was going, seeing the hobbling figure of a man from the wave ahead just a couple of hundred metres in front is something that will always get the legs pumping a bit faster. I overtook a man, and then I overtook another man. I pondered for a while: is the reason I haven't overtaken any women due to the small size of the field in relation to the men or because women generally haven't embraced triathlon as something to 'just have a go at' in the same way that men have? The sight of a woman ahead of me interrupted that train of thought. I overtook her with 400 m to go, offering my encouragement as I went past. Katie, who'd now had ample time to go back to her car and get changed, was stood by the finishing line shouting out at me. I'd finished in a total time of 3 hours 32 minutes. Somebody has to come last. But this time at least, it wasn't me.

KATIE

Takeaway training advice: Preparing for your first triathlon

How you train for your first triathlon, and how long the training takes, is dependent on so many things: your current fitness levels; your aptitude and confidence in each of the three disciplines; the race distance you plan to tackle; and what your goals are, to name a few. With three sports, and so many distances available, there are lots of variables and there is certainly no one-size-fits-all approach to training. There are plenty of 'off the peg' training programmes available on the Internet but it's important to bear in mind that they won't take into account where your relative strengths and weaknesses lie. Laura came to triathlon with an established background in running but had to learn to swim from scratch before her first race, so she allowed time to build confidence in the water and cover the distance. Laura's training focus could look a lot different to that of a strong swimmer who hasn't trained since they were a teenager and feels daunted by the thought of a

5 km run. These differences are something that makes triathlon accessible to so many people, but they can also make it look more complicated than it really is at first. Writing a generic training plan in this book would be as useful as including a takeaway menu, so, instead, here are some training ideas explained to help get you on your way.

Despite the misleading term 'sprint triathlon', the vast majority of triathlons are endurance events, which means you'll need to be ready to keep going over a period of time. A sprint triathlon takes the elites about an hour, so the rest of us can expect to spend a little longer than that. If your goal is simply to finish, then your training may simply build towards covering the distances confidently: your training could start with the distance you can cover comfortably in each discipline, however short that might be, and work on extending this gradually over time. If your goal is to go faster, even if just in your strongest discipline, then you may wish to build some more intensity into your sessions. Among the longer, steadier sessions, many training plans will include something known as 'interval' training, which are sessions that alternate hard efforts with rest periods and help improve speed and cardiovascular fitness. The speed or intensity that you do these interval efforts at is important – too fast and your training becomes less relevant to endurance events, too gentle and you won't see much benefit – so seeking the advice of the coaches at your local triathlon club is recommended if you're new to this type of training. Whatever you decide to do, remember that it's better to start conservatively. Build up your training gradually, rather than leaping in with too much, too soon, and burning out within the first two weeks, wishing we'd included that takeaway menu after all.

Making a splash

Bike and run fitness don't translate particularly well to swimming so, whatever your swimming is like, swim fitness comes from time in the water. A new swimmer's aim may simply focus on building up to covering the distance for your event; however, if you're targeting an open-water event, remember also to include some time spent practising the skills specific to this such as sighting, swimming with other people around you, and even taking your wetsuit on and off. The same is true for more accomplished swimmers, although including some interval training will help to improve your swimming fitness. I'm rarely happier than when splashing around the lake in the summer but it does more for my soul than it does for my swimming speed; so some fitness sessions in the pool help to balance this out. A local triathlon club training session is a great place to start if you're new to the idea of more structured swimming sessions; aside from the fitness benefits, the more varied approach to training and the company of other swimmers are both great for maintaining motivation.

If I'm training at the pool alone, an example of a simple session structure might be:

- A 250 m warm-up with some technique drills.

- A few 200 m efforts at a harder pace with 20 seconds rest between each.

- A 250 m cool-down swim, focusing on technique (for example, I try to concentrate on exhaling fully).

Swimming session plans are normally given in metres, so that different length pools can be used. The website www. swimsmooth.com is a great resource for triathlon-specific swim training advice and it offers a pace calculator to help you pace your intervals and get maximum benefit from your time in the water.

Swimming is arguably the most technical of the three sports in triathlon and, if you are learning to swim from scratch, then your swimming teacher is going to be giving you lots of feedback and tips for improvement on your stroke. Make the most of all this feedback as it can be harder to come by when you graduate from your lessons. More experienced swimmers tend to lack this input yet could make some big improvements with just a little bit of brushing up on technique. Many triathlon clubs are lucky enough to have qualified coaches at swim sessions so don't be afraid to ask for their advice. If you want to push the boat out, attending a swimming workshop or clinic with some video analysis is a very powerful way to learn what you look like when you swim and how to make some changes that will improve your stroke. One or two key cues to think about when you're swimming can keep you focused on your form, and help maintain technique, particularly as you tire. In my experience, the less dignified the cue, the more memorable the image, so don't be a prude. A coach recently told me to think about holding a £2 coin between my bum cheeks, to help maintain a good leg position in the water. Come to think of it, a running coach also told me to run like there's a credit card in the same place, which makes me quite grateful that there are pockets in my cycling jersey to carry loose change on bike rides.

Cycle of success

If you're very new to cycling then the priority will be to become confident on your bike and gradually increase the distance so that you are happy you can complete your event in one piece. Nothing beats riding in the great outdoors when it comes to learning the skills of riding, how to handle your bike on corners and downhills, and, of course, falling in love with cycling. In the next two chapters, we'll talk through some ways to increase the mileage on your bike.

Increasing the intensity of your cycle training can be done by throwing in some harder efforts during a ride, say five x 5 minutes of harder work, or finding some hills to get your heart rate up; this is best achieved once you are more confident on your bike. Winter, rain, dark evenings or long days in the office can all make cycling less tempting than normal so, if you can't face wrapping yourself in several layers, a more appealing option is to stay inside. This doesn't have to mean you stop pedalling as there are options for indoor cycling. For a new cyclist, this can also be a good way to add an interval session in to your week without worrying about cornering and avoiding potholes.

Indoor cycling classes: many gyms will offer indoor cycling classes, often known as 'spin' classes, where an instructor will lead you through a structured training session of 45–60 minutes in length; more and more dedicated cycle studios are popping up, specialising in these classes alone. If it's the difference between cycling or not, then having an instructor to help motivate you, music to distract you, and a structured training session that you didn't need to think about, can be a good way to break up training, certainly through the winter months. Bear in mind that the way that some stationary bikes work means that you may be working your hamstrings more than the muscle groups you'd use riding on the road, and the fit and dimensions of the stationary bike will differ to your own, so make sure this isn't the only source of your cycle training.

Turbo trainers: indoor cycling can get pretty sweaty. If you're conscious of the puddle accumulating around your spin bike, or put off by the thought of 20 other sticky cyclists in such close proximity to you, you might like to invest in a turbo trainer: a piece of kit to which you attach the frame of your own bike so that your rear wheel can move against a rolling resistance unit. Starting at around £60, you can turn your bike into an indoor cycle and pedal away to your heart's content, listening to tunes of your own choosing and in the comfort of your own home. A very simple interval session could take the form of a 10 minute warm-up, followed by alternating 5 minutes of sustained effort and 5 minutes easy pedalling, repeated for an hour. If you miss the company of a spin instructor shouting at you, you can download training podcasts, such as Chrissie Wellington's 'Ride Harder' from Audio Fuel, and follow a guided session. You will get pretty hot so grab a bottle of water and put a small towel over your handlebars and stem to stop salty sweat dropping on your bike and causing it to go rusty. If you're setting your trainer up inside your house, put a towel on the floor to protect it and open the windows. I have my turbo trainer set up out in the garden shed with a big fan to blow cold air from outside. It works well but I have to be careful when I reach for my water bottle: if it's sitting on the shelf next to a bottle of screen wash and weed killer, the training session can become a game of rehydration Russian roulette.

Building bricks: bike to run

There is no escaping the fact that going running straight after a bike ride feels horrible. It really does. Your legs are used to pedalling round in circles, not pounding the ground; meanwhile, your bum is perched up on a saddle with relatively little to do. Those lovely big muscles in your backside, that are so important for running, have nodded off while your quads do the nightshift. Then, suddenly, the alarm clock rings and they're expected to take over; it's like waking a teenager in the school holidays and asking them to do extra maths homework. In my case, my hamstrings seem to do the lion's share, leaving my running gait looking less like elegant forward motion and more like two heavy legs trying to push the world backwards underneath my feet, with all thoughts of that credit card long forgotten.

There is a key training session that can make the transition less of a nightmare. It's very simple in principle – you go for a run after a bike ride – but it's so notorious it gets its own name in triathlon street lingo: the 'brick session'. Word. One of the perceived physiological benefits of this session is simply the idea that you practise running with good form, which helps activate those muscles that have gone to sleep after sitting on a saddle for a while. I know I look and feel like an elderly hen in flip flops when I get off the bike and I try to start running; the more I can do to practise putting this right, the better. Psychologically, practising something that you know is difficult and conquering it makes perfect sense. The fact that your legs will feel dreadful might sound like a scary proposition to recreate in training, but I've found that brick sessions get less uncomfortable the more you do them.

Luckily, brick sessions are quite easy to fit into your training. A short run of 10–15 minutes after a bike ride or indoor cycle session, no more than once a week, will start to get your legs used to the changeover. You could work towards completing a 5 km run as part of a brick session, three or four weeks before your race, to help your confidence on race day. Make it as straightforward as possible by putting your trainers by the door (or the treadmill, if you're at the gym) so that you can go straight out; it's a good opportunity to integrate a quick transition practice too.

Dear Diary...

Whatever your approach to training, consider keeping a simple diary of your sessions. It's useful to keep track of your balance between the three sports and the type of sessions you have been doing. You can also use it to monitor when you've felt at your best and when you've felt at your worst. If you've been feeling particularly fatigued then make a note and dial the training back a little until you're feeling perkier again. A training diary can be as simple as a little notebook with your sessions written down, or whatever works for you. Laura uses Post-it notes to keep times from her interval sessions quickly to hand and keep track of her progress. I sometimes use a wall planner in the run up to a big race as it helps me to see patterns and progression over a number of weeks; I can also see where I've got other commitments coming up and spot if gaps are appearing in my training. Training plans are one thing but a note of what you actually did is a great way of tracking your own progress; not to mention a useful thing to look back on if and when you plan your next event.

Some useful training resources

www.britishtriathlon.org

The British Triathlon Federation website can help you to find a triathlon club in your area.

www.beginnertriathlete.com

This site offers a wide selection of free downloadable triathlon training plans for different distances. Some of them are quite involved, suggesting more hours of training than you may be ready to commit to, so be selective.

www.swimsmooth.com/training

Swim Smooth offers a great swimming pace calculator for interval training and lots of really useful triathlon-specific swimming advice.

www.mcmillanrunning.com

A great site that uses a race time to calculate guide paces for running interval sessions.

www.audiofuel.co.uk/chrissie-wellington

Audio Fuel sells a selection of triathlon training podcasts recorded by four-times World Ironman Champion, Chrissie Wellington. Sessions include running and indoor cycling, as well as relaxation and motivation sessions.

LAURA

A moveable feast:
Fig rolls and long bike rides

For four years I'd entered the London Marathon ballot and for four years I'd been rejected. So, when I put my name in the hat for the first ever Ride London–Surrey 100 cycle sportive, I didn't think too much about the implications. When a magazine dropped through my door to tell me that I'd got a place to cycle 100 miles, I decided to give it a go because it started at the Queen Elizabeth Olympic Park, which sounded a bit fun and I needed to cycle 100 miles to put me off the silly idea I had about doing an iron-distance triathlon. The event took place at the start of August and, by July, the furthest I'd ever cycled was 26 miles and that involved a pizza and beer stop part way round. It was time to seek help from Katie.

To say I hadn't done any training at all would be a lie. I'd been on my bike at least four days a week for most of the year, cycling to and from work in all weathers. Snow, rain, heatwaves, wind – you name it, I'd cycled through it. I clocked up 10 miles a day on a bike commute and had to cycle up a decent hill on the way home. Long cycles, however, had been lacking. The longest cycle I'd done that didn't involve a beer and pizza stop was the 24 miles that had been sandwiched between a 1,500 m swim and a 10 km run at the Marlow Triathlon in June.

One thing I've learnt over the years is that it's great hanging around people that have raced much further distances than you're attempting – it makes your stupid, over-ambitious plans look more achievable. Katie knows a bit about cycling. She's cycled from John O' Groats to Land's End before. That's quite far. Much further than I needed to cycle. So I took my bike on the train to Oxford to visit Katie and hoped the cycle she planned to take me on was a little more modest. On what was one of the hottest Saturdays the UK has experienced in recent years, three of us (me, Katie and Anita – another speedy cyclist) headed out into the Oxfordshire countryside. I'd brushed up on proper cyclists hand signals before I went. The hand signals cyclists do in London are very different to those that you'll find in a cycling handbook. I learned about the flappy one-winged bird sign that means slow down and that making a circle with your finger pointing at the ground signifies a pothole or other hazard. It's little surprise that I hadn't come across these on my cycle commute – my arms would do more work than my legs if I gestured for each and every pothole on my way home from work.

'I thoroughly believe the key to cycling longer is to get out of London,' Katie had emailed me.

She was right. Without any traffic or stop signs, the miles flew by. And I had a couple of friends to chat to as we went. My chat was something along the lines of, 'I'm sure this village was in *Midsomer Murders*. And this one. And this one. Is that

DCI Barnaby?' Soon enough there was no chatter coming from any of us as we reached something called Brill Hill. As names go, this one is as misleading as they get. It was not brill, at least not as far as my legs were concerned. I puffed my way to the top, trailing behind the other two, careful to balance my speed so it wasn't quite so slow that I would come to a complete stop and fall off.

I'm from the Fens. I'm not meant for going up and down hills, certainly not on a bike. In my first term at university in Loughborough, I needed to get to the library to collect a book before it closed. A friend loaned me his bike so I could get there quicker, so I set off to ride the 2 miles to the library. Loughborough isn't a place noted for its hills, but as I cycled towards the library, I had to ride up, what seemed like, a mountain to me. Halfway up I had to get off the bike and push it. I returned to my halls with the bike and the book, moaning about the massive hill. Nobody knew what I was talking about and they were convinced I'd gone to the wrong library – they saw the campus as flat. If they came to the Fens they'd know the true meaning of the word flat.

At the top of Brill Hill I collapsed onto a bench and, once I'd regained the ability to talk, I conceded that, yes, it did have quite a brill view. Katie cycled off to fetch ice creams and cans of cold drinks. This, I agreed, was one thing that cycling had over running – the ability to stop for ice cream and fizzy drinks, even beer. Twenty-eight miles into our cycle my ears pricked up as Katie called back over her shoulder, 'Want to stop at the pub?' It was met with a very enthusiastic: 'YES! I thought you'd never ask.' There were just 2 miles to go which meant another delicate balancing act – how much can we drink and still cycle back safely?

On the morning of Ride London, I set my alarm for 5 a.m. and cycled with my colleague, Tom, to the Olympic Park where the ride would start. As we cycled through the streets of East London, we passed people making their way home from a night out, staggering along to catch a bus home and had to swerve round smashed bottles and glasses in the road. A puncture before we'd already started was not on the agenda. Ride 100 had a strict cut-off time of 9 hours. If you didn't meet certain checkpoints by certain times you'd be asked to leave the course and put on the sweeper bus so the roads could be kept clear for the elite race, which was setting off a few hours after the mass event and would make quick work of making up ground. A puncture was my biggest fear and would put me in real danger of a ride on the sweeper bus – that and three massive hills.

Katie texted me as I got into my start pen: 'Remember to keep eating and you'll be fine.' The day before I'd packed myself a picnic. I loaded the pockets of my cycle jersey and my tiny crossbar picnic hamper with nine fig rolls, two cheese sandwiches and two Snickers bars. While I stood waiting in the Olympic Park to join 16,000 other cyclists to ride 100 miles, I cracked open the first of the fig rolls. I looked around at my fellow picnickers. Some were clearly anticipating being much less hungry than me.

A horn sounded and signalled the start of my 100 mile picnic: we were off. Cycling along traffic-free streets, past the Tower of London, through Trafalgar Square and past Harrods felt really special. We made our way west and, before I knew it, we were entering Richmond Park having gone through 20 miles and four fig rolls. Tom and another colleague, who'd started in a later wave, cycled up alongside me and we had a chat before they sped off ahead. A few miles after that a Welsh guy turned his iPhone on and Bob Marley echoed from his handlebars; we had a brief chat and then he too cycled off. There was a theme occurring.

Twenty-five miles in and my bum started to hurt. A lot. How I would complete three quarters of the race with a painful bum was beyond me. But after the first significant hill at Newlands, I hopped off my bike to use a Portaloo and eat the first of my Snickers. I had a chat with a guy from the West Midlands, took a photo, and climbed back into the saddle a bit less sore for the break.

Leith Hill was next. At 136 metres high and 1.24 miles long, it was bigger and steeper than the first hill and every time I thought I was at the top, the road would turn and the hill continued. The road was narrow and when an emergency vehicle came up behind us, I stopped to let it pass and had to walk the last 50 metres. At the top, cyclists were laid out on the side of the road resting; it seemed as good a place as any to stop. I looked at my watch and decided that I'd made good enough time to allow me to have a break. So I took out my first cheese sandwich and sat on the curb to eat it. After half an hour's break from my saddle, I didn't fancy climbing back on but the descent looked appealing. The road dropped away beneath us as we sped down the other side of the hill and I told myself, Don't brake, don't brake, don't brake, OK brake, brake, BRAKE! There were a couple of accidents but nobody seemed too badly injured.

Box Hill, 141 metres high, loomed in the distance as we made our way towards the last big climb of the day. I drained the last from my drinks bottles and turned right onto the slope. And it wasn't that bad. We were 65 miles in so climbing wasn't great, but taking it steady I climbed slowly, reading the graffiti on the road that had been there for the past year, originally written to cheer on Cav and Wiggo in the Olympic Road Race. At the top of Box Hill, the hard part of the day was over. I took a photo, took photos for other elated cyclists, and sat down to eat my second sandwich. By now, I was confident that I'd be able to avoid a ride on the sweeper bus and I was in no rush to move off from the top of the hill. It was a good day to be up there looking out across the Surrey countryside and it was a good day to be a cyclist.

Eventually I climbed onto my bike for the last time and zoomed off down the hill, munching what remained of my picnic as we headed back towards London. From 70 miles, I knew the route well and it passed places I'd lived. We headed through Kingston, where the crowd cheered as though we were the pros; and through Wimbledon, past people sat drinking outside my old local, cheering us on and back over the river towards the finish.

Ironically, as the road was closed to traffic, I sped along the last few miles towards the Houses of Parliament in the cycle lane. The smooth blue tarmac felt faster than the rest of the road so I clung tightly to the edge of the road. We turned into Trafalgar Square again and this time we went under Admiralty Arch and onto The Mall. The crowd roared as we headed towards the finishing line and I high-fived a cyclist riding alongside me. I finished in 7 hours 48 minutes, which surprised me, but more importantly, I was quicker than Boris Johnson and the sweeper bus. Now I had to get back home to North London and the only way there was by bike. By the time I added on the cycle home from the race and the ride to the start I'd clocked up around 112 miles. Which is, coincidentally, the length of an ironman bike leg. But there was no chance of me pulling on my running shoes that day.

KATIE

Chamois, shorts and shelter: Your guide to cycling further

'But where does it go?' I asked my friend.

Two novice cyclists looked quizzically at a pot of Vaseline before setting off on a bike ride from John O' Groats to Land's End.

'I have no idea but I've heard it's essential,' she replied.

We put the little pot back into our bag and decided that, if it really were necessary, it would become clear what to do with it before too long. By the end of our first day, we agreed that sharing the contents would no longer be appropriate and stopped to buy another.

There are places on a bicycle where friction and pressure are very good things: your brakes would be useless without the former; without the latter, your tyres would be flat and you'd be left riding along on a once-round pair of aluminium rims. There is one place in particular where we could do without these two scientific phenomena though; I refer to mine politely as the 'Bike-Lady Interface'. Gentlemen, you may call yours what you please, but you have an 'interface' too. In the interests of clarity, I've drawn a diagram:

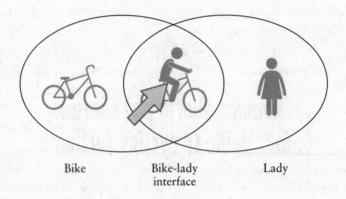

Bike   Bike-lady   Lady
interface

With a little more experience, I now know that the pot of petroleum jelly is not actually necessary at all, but what I cannot do without is a good saddle and a decent pair of cycling shorts. Think beyond the 1990s fashion frenzy, I'm talking about the ones with a nice padded chamois (pronounced 'shammy', like 'jammy') stitched in.

Many new cyclists despair at the idea of wearing them and there is no getting away from the fact that, the first time you put them on, it feels like there's the crust of a thick-sliced wholemeal loaf down your shorts. But if you think that's uncomfortable, try riding for more than 2 hours without a pair: your lady garden will be blooming in black and blue, or the fruits of your man orchard overripe and bruised. Now who's uncomfortable?

I know you'll see those professional triathletes winning an iron-distance race in nothing more than what looks like a wafer thin pair of pants; this has always baffled me, to be perfectly honest. I can only assume that their saddles are stitched from the delicate underbelly of a centaur and woven together with fairy dust; that, or their undercarriage is undergoing a certain degree of 'compromise' over the course of a 112-mile bike ride. We mere mortals need more protection down there. Don Fink talks about being 'comfortable with the uncomfortable' in his long-distance triathlon bible, *Be Iron Fit*, but I thought he was talking about running a marathon at that point and not the contents of his shorts. Take one look at the pro-cyclists: hard as nails but never a chamois shunned. When Sir Dave Brailsford (Principal of Team Sky and former Performance Director at British Cycling) talks about the theory of 'marginal gains' in his squad's training methods and technology, I'd like to think that he's also referring to that extra few millimetres of wadding in the shorts of his athletes, and the savings he makes on his Savlon bill.

There are different styles of shorts available: for men, for women, bibs (like braces but cosier), no bibs (easier for toilet trips), baggies (for mountain bikers, or shy people), or ones with skirts attached (please don't). For triathlons, 'tri suits' or their little brothers, the tri short, have a slightly less industrial-looking chamois than regular cycling shorts; this means that you don't soak up the contents of the pool and cause a monsoon from your shorts as you land on your saddle. They all have the same purpose: keeping your interface happy. Once you've chosen your pair, you're ready to go.

Just one thing though: leave your pants at home. Cycling and triathlon have just been added to your list of knickerless recreational activities, since the seams of your undergarments just add to the risk of chafing. Suddenly, a little bit of chamois allows you to fly in the face of convention and parade around without your smalls on, how liberating! This does restrict your kit wearing to a strict one wear/one wash laundry pattern but I think it's worth it.

If all that hasn't convinced you, let me leave you with one last point. A European directive, known as 'Chamois Time', dictates that any time spent in cycling kit counts as time spent on the bike. Today, for example, I rode my bike for 4.5 hours. Since then, I've eaten lunch, drunk a coffee, and written this chapter, all while wearing my shorts: that's another 2 hours of training for free! I'll leave you to ponder that as I go and put some washing on.

Upping the mileage

While shorts are imperative as you start to ride further, they won't stand up and turn the pedals for you, even if you don't adhere to the one wear policy. 'Winter miles make summer smiles,' say cyclists through the bleakest months of the year. When our winter seems to last ten months, that's easier said than done though; I know I can be pretty late to the pedal party if spring is wetter than an otter's pocket. If distance is something you're looking to increase with a longer distance triathlon in mind then here are some tips for upping your mileage in training:

Kit up

No matter how far you are venturing on your bike in training, there are some essentials to carry with you as you go. A cycling jersey with a couple of pockets in the back and a little bag attached under your saddle will allow you to carry items such as a map, food, mobile phone, money, a cycling multi-tool (this will have the basic Allen keys to fit most bolts on your bike) and a spare inner tube. If you learn only one mechanical skill as a cyclist, it should be how to remove your wheel to change an inner tube and re-inflate it to get home after a puncture.

Buddy up

I've never liked the phrase 'misery loves company'; however, I do believe that 'mileage loves company'. Cyclists hunt in packs, largely because the wind is our worst enemy and any shelter given by the rider in front can be sweet relief from a relentless breeze. Known as 'drafting', sitting behind another cyclist offers a significant reduction in the energy required to travel at the same speed without them there (though, remember that you won't be allowed to do this in your triathlon). Cycling with company has many other benefits too, not least someone to hold on to your bike while you go for a wee behind a hedge.

If you're feeling really keen, contact a local cycling club and ask to join them on a club ride. Group riding is a great skill to learn, not to mention way more fun, and some clubs will offer a beginners' ride with a leader to take care of the navigating. Bike skills learned while cycling in a group, such as cornering and riding downhill, will come in very handy for your triathlon. Cycling with other more experienced cyclists is also a great way to improve bike handling, up your mileage, and generally soak up the sport by osmosis. You never know, you might also be inspired to give cycling a go as a sport in its own right.

Fuel up

Nutrition is something to consider carefully on a long bike ride. What's known as 'hitting the wall' in marathon running is more affectionately known as 'bonking' by cyclists. The cause and effect remain the same, namely the depletion of your body's glycogen stores, and the punishing feeling that your legs have called it a day without consulting the rest of you. If you're not sure whether you've experienced it, you probably haven't; once you have, you'll do anything to avoid it again.

Fit a bottle cage to your bike so that you can take a bottle with you and practise riding with one hand so that you can drink from the bottle on the move. Even on short rides, it's good to sip from a bottle of water and you can replace it with a sports drink for a longer ride. Luckily, cycling has a distinct advantage over swimming and running: the ability to eat solids. Fig rolls, that well-known food of sporting champions and Laura's personal favourite, make excellent bite-size snacks that you can easily retrieve from your jersey pocket; muesli bars; jelly babies; or sports-specific energy bars and gels are all also possible sources of energy. Just be careful not to start munching at the bottom of a climb or you may feel like you'll never breathe again. Try to eat small amounts regularly (e.g. every 30 minutes) if you're riding for more than 60–90 minutes; and try to avoid getting to the point of feeling hungry. If in doubt, I remember my brother's wise words, 'That food is no good in your pocket, Katie.'

If you're heading out for a long day on your bike, why not take in a cafe stop? The elite may frown upon this but it's not cheating if it means you ride for longer than without; I would certainly never judge anyone stopping for a coffee.

Move up

Make the most of a long bike ride by thinking of it as an adventure; anything that takes you away from your usual routes can be considered as such and it's fun to find opportunities to cycle somewhere new. A holiday with your bike is a fairly committed way of doing this or a weekend away closer to home can also be an opportunity to explore new roads. You could take this one step further and even consider cycling there. I've arrived at hen weekends by bike, carrying a dress and a toothbrush in my little rucksack; this does take some level of understanding on the part of the bride-to-be, not to mention a fairly casual dress code, so choose your occasion wisely.

Burn it up

Bike rides don't always have to be long. A short, fast session has its own benefits and many believe that, in cycling, this may outweigh the benefits of really long, slow bike rides. Whether or not this is true, a fast 15 mile bike ride is much easier to fit into a working week than a long-distance crusade. Save the long rides for trying out new cafes with friends at the weekend and clocking up some valuable 'Chamois Time' in the process.

Running the Gauntlet: The Ironboy

'What training plan have you been using for your half-iron tri? I need a recommendation.'

'Training plan. Umm, I haven't really got one.'

'Oh, have you been using a coach?'

'No, none of those either.'

'Then how do you know how much training to do?'

'Well, I haven't exactly been training either. Not in the conventional sense.'

'OK, well good luck with your race then.'

This is a conversation I had a couple of weeks before my first half-iron distance debut. I was the party without a coach, training plan or traditional notion of what 'training' for a half-iron triathlon meant. Instead of training, I'd been 'preparing' for my race. This involved swimming, cycling and running, but in a more relaxed, unpressured and unmeasured sense than you'll see many triathletes adopt. Months before, when I signed up for my half-iron triathlon, I asked Katie to recommend a plan. She explained how she figured out her own training without the aid of such items but I persisted and so she gave me the name of a book that I read and I copied out the training plan from. I stuck it on my wall. And then I never looked at it again. The plan and I didn't get on. It wanted me to go for a run when I wanted to go swimming. It wanted me to rest when I wanted to cycle into work. And it wanted me to do a 3-hour cycle when I'd planned on cycling 90 miles from London to Peterborough in search of beer.

I was burned out from training for the Manchester Marathon earlier in the year. I didn't want to run. So I swam more, cycled every day, and forgot about my running shoes for a while. The plan told me to do certain swim workouts, but I was still working on being able to swim without stopping. It told me about heart rate zones and paces when I just wanted to plod along on my bike, forget my watch when I was running, and learn to love swimming outside. As the weeks went by, I 'trained' less and less but my amount of activity went up. Most days, I was either cycling 10 miles to work and back, splashing about in a pool or reservoir, heading to a yoga class, or doing some sort of relaxed running. I'd clocked up a lot of events too since my first triathlon; as well as the Ride 100 cycle, I'd done a couple of half marathons and some swim races. None of it, though, felt like training because I was doing it, not because a plan on my wall told me to, but because I wanted to. I switched between the three sports when I felt like it, so none of the three ever got tiresome and I looked forward to doing the other two while I was doing the third.

Some triathletes can be a bit obsessive to say the least. From training to nutrition to equipment, there are a lot of elements that can be measured, analysed and obsessed over. I didn't want to go down that road. It might help make me faster or fitter, but would it make me enjoy the sport more or would it just leave me anxious and stressed come race day? I took a wild guess and decided to leave all the obsessing over miles and calories and power output to those in front of me in the race.

My race was taking place in Kent around the picturesque setting of Hever Castle and was reassuringly called 'The Gauntlet'. Call me old fashioned, but I believe it's a good life rule to not enter races that involve words like hell, inferno, apocalypse or disemboweled. I forgot this when I signed up for my first half-iron distance tri. As the day approached, I felt prepared for the race through knowing that I'd done enough swimming, cycling and running to cope with the distances. I'd need to swim 1,900 metres, cycle 56 miles and run 13.1 miles. I'd done pretty much double the run and cycle distance in single sport events that year, and it was just the swim distance that would be new. That's not to say that the thought of doing them all at once didn't frighten me. It did. But the fact that I enjoyed every step, stroke and pedal of my preparation gave me confidence that on race day I could enjoy that too. Because 70.3 miles is an awfully long way to go if you're not having fun. And if the worst happened and I had to 'DNF', I hoped I wouldn't feel that the past few months had been wasted. Because every time I climbed on my bike or zipped up my wetsuit, I wasn't doing it because of that one day in September, I was doing it because that's what I wanted to do in that moment.

On the morning of the race, though, I felt unprepared. I rushed into the transition area later than most of the other competitors and fumbled around trying to organise my things ready for the swim to bike and bike to run transitions. An official was calling all Gauntlet competitors down to the water for the swim briefing and counting down the time to the closing of transition while I struggled to pull on my wetsuit and get my gear together. I found Katie, who was competing too, and we ran down the hill to the swim start together. But, as a man with a megaphone explained our route out across the lake and then back via a channel, I looked round at all the silver swim caps and realised I didn't have my own. While everyone else adjusted their wetsuits and goggles, I ran back up the hill towards transition – my hat was lying on the ground halfway back, near some Portaloos.

I made it back before the race began at 8 a.m., as a cannon fired and 300 competitors swam out into a lake for the 1.9 km swim leg. I watched the mass of swimmers head out across the lake. Katie was somewhere in among the scrum of flailing arms and legs, churning up the water and the mud from the bottom of the lake to render the water opaque. I put my face in and started swimming, hoping that I wouldn't swallow too much of the murky water.

After a hundred metres or so, the water got deeper and clearer. The lake was nice and wide and there was space for us at the back to swim without bashing into each other. At 200 metres in, something unusual happened: I caught up some of the other swimmers and had to start overtaking. This was uncharted territory for me. After 750 metres, we swam round a buoy and headed back on ourselves before swimming right down a channel. The channel went round an island where spectators were dotted about watching from the banks. I'm used to swimming in a wiggly line but usually when I should be going straight. Navigating the winding channel did make it interesting and different to your usual out and back swim. We swam under a bridge where spectators were looking down, waving at us, before turning one last corner that saw us heading back to where we'd started for the exit.

I set a new record for slowest transition ever, taking more than 8 minutes to get my wetsuit off and climb onto my bike. It was a combination of cold hands that didn't work properly and a reluctance to start cycling. I ambled through the first few miles over some rolling hills with a few cyclists passing me, but before long I was on my own again. Luckily, I'd come prepared with some mental games to play and lots of snacks to busy myself working through. But timing my picnic to coincide with the downhills became a game in itself.

The highest point of the course (at just over 200 metres) was halfway along the bike loop, and we'd do two laps. As I emerged from the trees of Ashdown Forest to see the peak on the first loop, I felt good that it hadn't been as hard as I thought it might be. The feeling was short-lived as the second half of the loop had two killer hills that seemed to go on forever. There was a standard and sprint distance triathlon going on as part of the event too. They'd started their swim after we'd finished ours and had a smaller bike loop. Not long after the second steep hill, the standard distance triathletes joined us as our courses merged. It was nice to be among other competitors after cycling so much by myself, but after a while I got fed up of them all overtaking me with such ease. We headed back to the castle to start the second loop and, before long, our routes went off in different directions.

After 45 miles of cycling up and down hills, I was broken. I dropped down into my lowest gear to begin the slow grind up a beast of a hill I'd already climbed once, more than 2 hours before, and I began to cry. It wasn't just tears but big fat sobs coming out of me. I didn't want to do it anymore. I was tired, I was sore and, although I knew I was going to finish the bike leg, I wasn't relishing the thought of spending more than 2 hours running once I climbed off my bike. I cried for the last 10 miles of the bike course, but I didn't stop. Getting off the bike and racking it in transition was a relief. I ran over to a friend supporting for a hug and sobbed, 'I don't want to do it'.

There was no doubt, though, that I could do it and that I would.

Cap and running shoes on, I headed out for the first of two laps of the run. The run was largely trail and, like the bike route, peppered with hills. I marched up the hills and ran the rest, and before long I started to enjoy myself. My legs had remembered how to run and my brain had remembered that it likes running. We ran through fields, past a pub where an aid station was fully stocked with everything you could hope to eat, around two castles and alongside lots of cheery marshals.

I began overtaking people and, once we got onto the second leg, I'd got into a comfortable routine of happily sprinting down hills, running across the flat and marching up the hills. With 3 km to go, I saw two women about 400 metres ahead of me and made it my mission to pass them. I ran past them with 1.5 km left to go and I could hear people cheering at the finishing line in the distance. I marched up one last, gravelly hill and flung myself down the other side towards the finishing line. Despite all the tears, 8 hours and 6 minutes after I started, I finished my half-iron triathlon with a smile on my face. Katie was waiting for me at the finish with a pint of beer.

Crossing the finishing line usually leads to the inevitable question: what next? I staggered to the hospitality tent, ate a veggie sausage in a burger bun, and drank a massive coffee. That's what was next and all I cared about at that moment. I hadn't planned much beyond the finish line at The Gauntlet. Even the journey home hadn't been thought through. Unbeknown to me the train line back to London was closed, so I crammed myself, my soggy wetsuit and my bike into Katie's car, followed by a different train, and the back of a black cab. One £30 taxi fare and the faint smell of wee emanating from my wetsuit later, I was back home with that question to consider. What next?

As I cycled round the bike course at The Gauntlet I'd questioned myself. Did I really want to put myself through doing a race twice the distance? Could I do it? For the last 10 miles of the bike, as I sobbed my way up hills, the answer was no. As I found my running legs and pegged it round the run course, that no became a maybe. And as I sat on my sofa a week later, taking a week off from any running, cycling or swimming, it became a yes.

There are no 'easy' half-ironman events, but it turns out that the one I did, with more than 1,400 metres of climb on the bike course and a hilly off-road run, was particularly hard. That gave me hope for what was about to come. Because I'd decided that in nine months' time I would be lining up to start Ironman UK in Bolton. The distance of the race (a 3.8 km swim, a 112 mile cycle and a 26.2 mile run) made me feel physically sick, the months of training required were pretty daunting and the cut-off times made the chances of me failing pretty high. But I would give it a go anyway.

I got a lot of congratulatory messages from friends after The Gauntlet. One I replied to with: 'It's amazing what you can achieve when you accept the high chance of failure and do it anyway.' I knew when I started all this triathlon business that there was a good chance I wouldn't be able to do it – that my swim would go badly, that my bike would get a puncture or a broken chain, that I would miss the cut-off times and be forced to pull out of the race. But I carried on regardless. Because I'm not scared of failure and there's no challenge in attempting stuff you know you can do.

KATIE

Leading the pack:
What to take to a triathlon

To: 'Laura Fountain'
Subject: All the gear, no idea

I'm about to try and find all my kit for The Gauntlet.
Just realised that I've been using the same list for every
race this year and it's getting a bit tatty. Now typing one
I can keep. This feels a bit serious.

To: 'Katie King'
Subject: RE: All the gear, no idea

I will write a list too. Or you could send me your one.
My current list is a scrap of paper that I write on when I
wake up in the middle of the night in a panic. That and
my left hand.

The sun is streaming through the blinds of my dining room window and I'm sat at an unusually, and unnervingly, tidy table. On a day off like today, I'd normally be outside enjoying this sunshine but, instead, I've vacuumed every floor in the house, cleaned the bathroom, and finally put a fortnight's worth of clean washing away where it belongs. I've even cleaned my bike. Why? I'm procrastinating. It's two days to go until my second iron-distance triathlon in July 2014, and just over a week until Laura tackles her first at Ironman Bolton. I'm supposed to be packing my kit bag.

A few years ago, I discovered a simple little trick to help with this process: keep the list you made for the last race you did. I have a notebook with several scrappy lists for races of different types and different distances, written in pencil, and scored through each time I've used them. A more organised friend then suggested I type up my lists and save them on my computer so that I can go to them afresh each time. One such document is saved on my desktop as, 'The bloody triathlon list'; I dread opening it, not because that's how I feel about the race, but because I know that this list is so long that it will take me several hours to locate all the stuff I have written on it.

Curious to know what I was taking to The Gauntlet, Laura asked me to send her my list. Bearing in mind I managed to fill a Renault Kangoo with belongings when I travelled to central France for that curtailed first attempt at an iron-distance event, it should hardly have surprised her that the list covered the best part of two pages and included, among others, items such as a short-sleeved cycling jersey, a long-sleeved cycling jersey, spare leggings, an iPad, and a dress; the latter was for a work function I was supposed to disappear to straight after the race, suggesting that packing is not the only area of my life where I try to cram too much in.

My name is Katie and I pack too much stuff for triathlons.

A few weeks ago, we pushed our bikes across Hyde Park to the start of an 'Olympic' distance race at the World Tri London. The night before, in Laura's flat, I'd become mildly panicked to learn that we'd be cycling 5 miles across London with just a blue drawstring race issue rucksack each, into which we had to pack everything we needed for the day. I tried to hide my nerves from Laura and casually packed, unpacked, folded, unfolded, squashed, packed, repacked, and discarded the majority of an extraordinary pile of belongings I'd toted to London in the boot of my car. As we ambled across the park on race morning, we were surrounded by other triathletes, many of whom were weighed down by large bags and plastic boxes balanced precariously on the crossbars of their bikes. 'But what do they have in there?' Laura asked. This was one question for which I didn't seem to have an answer. As Laura put it after the race, 'I was already wearing my tri suit, my bike was stocked with a drink and some fig rolls, I had my helmet on and was riding my bike, the only thing left to do was pack my wetsuit, trainers and not forget my goggles.' Simple.

This is an aspect of triathlon where Laura has become an unparalleled expert in her field. Travelling to most of her races without a car, she can pack all she needs into a backpack, including a comprehensive set of snacks for both the race and the train journey, and a change of clothes for the pub afterwards. The only thing that doesn't make it into the rucksack is her bike.

It hasn't always been quite this way for Laura. She recalls, 'For my first triathlon (a sprint) I took two pairs of socks – one for the cycle and one for the run. After all, they were socks, they wouldn't take up much space.' Socks might seem small and insignificant but Laura learned a big lesson at that race, 'As I came back from the cycle to rack my bike and get ready for the run, I looked at my socks. Should I swap, should I not? I stood motionless for a few seconds that seemed like an eternity. This was my error.' That little spare pair of socks introduced an unnecessary option for Laura when her mind needed to be clear for the task ahead. 'Same socks or new socks? Change or don't change? And when you've just cycled as fast as you can and are in a rush to get onto the next stage, decision-making is the last thing you should be doing.'

Knowing what you're going to eat, drink, wear, and change into is invaluable in an event that, by its very nature, contains many variables, and taking along too many extra belongings can add in extra decisions that need to be made. 'It's tempting to take lots of different kit and nutrition options with you,' says Laura, 'it can make you feel reassured when you're packing that you have everything you could possibly need and delay making difficult decisions. But packing is when you need to be making those decisions – not when your brain is frazzled on exhaustion or adrenaline.'

We've mentioned lots of different pieces of kit in various places throughout this book but, unless you're making notes, what you probably want now is a simple list of what to pack for race day. So we've tried to put together a checklist of 'bare essentials' that will get you through your first sprint triathlon without incurring an excess baggage surcharge.

The Essentials

- Tri suit – or whatever it is that you're going to wear to swim in and keep on throughout the race.

- Sports bra – if necessary, put this on under your tri suit and wear it for the whole event. Some women's tri suits come with one already 'installed' but many women find they prefer a bit more upholstery than what this offers.

- Wetsuit – for open-water events only.

- Goggles.

- Swimming hat – if you're given one at the race, you may not even need your own, or you could double up in open water.

- Towel for transition – place this on the floor to dry your feet on.

- Trainers – as well as completing the run, you can ride a bike in running shoes if you don't want to commit to using cycling shoes. Remember to leave them untied in transition, or use an alternative such as elastic laces (see The Desirables list).

- Bike.

- Helmet – compulsory for all triathlons.

- Fuel and hydration – what you take depends on the length of your race, conditions on the day, and what you have tried and tested in training. A bottle of water or energy drink can be placed into the bottle cage on the bike, and a bar or gel placed in a tri suit pocket or with your kit in transition.

- Race number/stickers/timing chip – attached to your kit (and, possibly, bike and helmet), as instructed by the organiser.

- Safety pins – to pin your race number to your top or race belt (see The Desirables).

- Something to carry your belongings in to transition – this could be as simple as a carrier bag but you may see some people using a plastic box to help keep things organised; just bear in mind that the latter can be tricky to carry on a bike and may not be allowed in transition at some events.

And that's it. As you'll soon realise in triathlon, the sky really is the limit with kit and it's important not to panic when you rack your bike next to someone in transition who appears to be setting up a small retail outlet. That said, there are a few added extras that you may want to consider if you're likely to be doing more triathlons:

The Desirables

- Old flip flops – for walking from transition to the start of an open-water swim.

- Lubricant – to help get the wetsuit on and off.

- Waterproof suncream – Laura swears by P20; I just swear when I get it in my eyes.

- Cycling shoes – if you're planning to do more cycling/triathlon, then moving into cycling shoes and clip-in pedals is a wise move that you won't regret.

- Elastic laces/lace locks – to put your running shoes on as fast as possible, you may want to avoid tying and untying laces.

- Stop watch/GPS – if you find that kind of thing helpful. Just remember to consider beforehand whether you'll want to be messing around with buttons for lap times, or how you're going to start it in a swim mass start.

- Sunglasses – useful in the sun, and for keeping the flies out of your eyes on the bike. Cycling specific sunglasses tend to 'wraparound' in style since they'll allow more vision to the sides and protection from bugs and grit; good vision and comfort should be your priorities, although I like a pair that are light enough to stay put when running too.

- Race belt – this is just a fancy piece of sturdy elastic onto which you can pin your race number. If the organiser only gives you one number, this becomes an essential item since you can move the number to the back while you're cycling and to the front for the run. What makes it fancy is a plastic buckle, which you use to fasten the belt around your waist in transition; however, if you really want to improvise, you could always make your own with a thick piece of elastic, wide enough to pin a number to, knotted into a loop big enough that you can step into it and tight enough that it stays around your waist. Just call me Kirstie Allsopp and be done with it.

● Visor or cap – again for keeping the sun out of your eyes on the run. Once asked why she wears one, Laura replied, 'It seems silly after wearing a swim cap and a helmet not to complete a hat-wearing triathlon too.'

The list can go on and on but these basics should get you through the early days until you've worked out what works specifically for you at races. Ultimately, the kit you use and decide to take is down to personal preference and budget, the weather forecast, and the type of race you'll be doing. The minimal approach can work well for shorter races but you'll have a different set of needs (and, possibly, shorts) for an iron-distance race. I might pack enough kit into my car for three sports, for three days and three people, but by the time I walk into transition, I've whittled it down to exactly what I need and I know what I'll be wearing and when I'll be wearing it. If you genuinely want to use two pairs of socks, take two pairs of socks; just think it through before you find yourself standing in transition, with sweat in your eyes, staring blankly at them, and wondering where they go.

Back in my dining room, it's a good job I've done some tidying up. 'The bloody triathlon list' is ready on my computer and there'll be kit all over the place in a few minutes time. What I realise from Laura's advice is the thing I'm really putting off is the decision-making ahead of race day; often I find that this can be one of the more difficult aspects of my triathlon and, if I get this bit sorted, then the rest is in the bag, so to speak. As my dining room floor becomes covered in triathlon kit, I won't just think about my event this weekend, but Laura's plans too; she's ready for her iron-distance triathlon in more ways than she realises.

To: 'Laura Fountain'
Subject: RE: All the gear, no idea
Attachment: THE BLOODY TRIATHLON LIST.doc

To: 'Katie King'
Subject: RE: All the gear, no idea

That has just given me palpitations!

KATIE

Hard and fast:
What are the rules in triathlon?

Sometimes it feels like there are a lot of rules in triathlon. Most are for your safety and many are borne out of common sense, which makes them easy to remember; however, some are a little stranger so it's worth being aware of the main ones so that you don't get caught out on race day. Here is a guide to some of the main triathlon rules (for a more extensive set of rules, go to the British Triathlon Federation website, or check with the organisers for races outside the UK).

Triathlon unplugged

Nothing that could impede your concentration or hearing is allowed during the race; this includes music players and headphones. Leave your mobile in your kit bag and save your selfies for after the race.

Leave your rubber duck at home

Swimming caps and goggles are allowed in the swim, and if you are provided with a cap by the event organisers, you must wear it; however, no rubber rings, floats, lilos, or flippers are allowed, so keep your bath toys on dry land. Wetsuits, which help with buoyancy, are optional in open water at certain temperatures. Above these temperatures, they are forbidden to prevent you overheating. The temperature at which you can and can't wear your suit depends on the length of the swim.

Swim distance	Water temperature below which wetsuits are compulsory	Water temperature above which wetsuits are banned
Up to 1,500 metres	14°C	22°C
1,501–3,000 metres	15°C	23°C
3,001–4,000 metres	16°C	24°C

Source: British Triathlon Federation

Keep your kit on

Triathlon is not a fan of nudity. Your upper body must be covered for the cycle and run, and any front fastening tri suits and tops must be zipped up. Neither bare chests nor bare feet are allowed during the run.

Keep your hands to yourself

No deliberate obstruction or interference with other competitors is permitted during any part of the race. There are bound to be a few knocks in an open-water swim but anything other than accidental contact is forbidden.

A numbers game

Your number must be visible at all times during the race; many organisers help you to achieve this by providing more stickers than the clearance aisle in Tesco. In particular, your main race number must be displayed on your back during the cycle and on your front during the run.

Working order

Your bike must be well-maintained and roadworthy, with brakes on both wheels working well. Handlebars need plugs in the ends; if you crash, an empty bar end can act like a cookie cutter so plugs avoid that happening. A race official will check your bike before you can enter transition.

Head first

A cycle helmet must be worn for the bike leg, with chinstrap fastened snugly. Sometimes, race officials will even check this by asking you to wear your helmet to rack your bike before the race. During the race, you must fasten your helmet before taking your bike from the rack; likewise, your helmet can only be removed after the bike has been returned to its rack before the run.

On your bike

You must push your bike out of transition and you can only get on once you are past the marked 'mount line' outside transition. You must also dismount where you are asked to before entering the second transition. When you're out on the road, obey the normal rules of the Highway Code and listen and respond to the instructions of police and marshals.

Stay out of the draft

Most events are 'draft illegal', which means that you are not allowed to take shelter behind or next to another cyclist. Each cyclist has an imaginary rectangle around them at any point on the bike course, called the 'draft zone', which measures 7 m back from the front wheel and 3 m wide (long distance events have a larger zone). An overtaking cyclist can only move into the rectangle of another competitor if they are clearly moving forwards through the zone. If you are being overtaken, you must drop out of the draft zone of the cyclist in front before you can re-attempt overtaking. Drafting rules apply to vehicles too so stay back from that ice cream van, however tempting it might be.

Keep transition tidy

Space can be at a premium in transition so keep it neat. If your bike or kit is left in anyone else's way then you can receive a time penalty. You are also not allowed to mark your place in transition, so save the balloons and streamers for that celebratory selfie after the finish. Since space can be limited, only competitors are allowed into transition; this is also for the security of your bike and kit.

Do it yourself

Triathlon is, by nature, an individual sport, so working together with any other competitors to provide an advantage to you or them is not allowed. Competitors are also not allowed to receive assistance, other than from the event officials; this includes food and drink from supporters, or lifts in the back of a van.

Play nicely

Triathlon may be an individual sport but 'individual' doesn't exclude the consideration of others. The BTF rules state that, 'All competitors, officials and volunteers and spectators must be treated with respect and courtesy'. In an ideal world, it shouldn't even need to be a rule. Ultimately, the rules of triathlon are there to promote a safe and sporting atmosphere, and to simply make it fair for all; it's your responsibility to follow them and make your race safe and fair for everyone. Be nice and have fun.

 **LAURA**

Once bitten, twice tri:
Learning to love triathlon
in my second season

Ironman training began on 24 December 2013: I got out of bed and the 30-week journey began. My laidback approach to training schedules had got me through the half-iron distance but, for the Ironman, I planned a more structured training regime. While people headed out to do some last minute Christmas shopping, I headed to Peterborough Regional Swimming Pool, where I remembered swimming as a child before getting fish and chips on the way home. I hadn't been back there for more than ten years. It'd had a few coats of paint since then but the smell was exactly the same.

I swam up and down for half an hour in the pool where I once struggled to do more than a couple of lengths. Then I hit the showers. In the afternoon, I put on my trainers and headed out into the wind for 400 m repeats before going out with my family for a traditional Christmas Eve curry and a few pints that were followed by repeats of a different kind. On Boxing Day, my dad and I headed off for a 10-mile run (me running, him on the bike) but this was cut short at 1.5 miles. I had my period and stomach cramps that got worse and worse through the first mile until I was crouched down on the ground groaning in agony. This was unfortunate news for both my dad and me; I commandeered his bike for the 1.5 mile return journey forcing him to do the running.

Friday started with another 9 a.m. swim, cut short just 20 minutes into it with another strategic attack from my uterus. I retreated to the sofa – Ironman training wasn't off to the best of starts, but I fought back on the Saturday morning by heading to the Peterborough parkrun. It was an icy cold morning and I turned up wearing a long sleeve top and a jumper, feeling quite inadequate next to club runners in the club vests and shorts. As we headed off round Ferry Meadows Country Park for a couple of laps of the lake, I was still wearing all the layers I came in and still felt cold. There was ice on the path so the choice was to risk slipping over or getting wet feet running on the grass. I straddled the edge of both and managed to keep upright. As we came round for the end of the first lap, I'd taken off my jumper and was running hard. My dad shouted out that I was doing well and something else that I couldn't quite catch. As we rounded the lake for the second time, I looked ahead round the edge of the lake at the competitors ahead of me and realised he'd been shouting that I was first lady. I'd never been first at anything and, although parkrun isn't a race per-se, it would still be nice to be the first woman to finish. I looked back over my shoulder as we rounded the corners for the last mile. A young female club runner was making up ground but there wasn't enough course left for her to catch up all the way. She finished 10 seconds or so behind me.

The next day, I said goodbye to my family and the luxury of not having to fit work in around my training and headed back to London to a late Christmas gift in the shape of a turbo trainer. The plan was to fight bad weather with indoor cycling and to keep my legs pedalling despite snow and ice. With just 30 minutes of fast pedalling in front of the TV, week one of Ironman training was done – there were just 29 to go.

As I'd hurtled along a bumpy road on my bike during the Marlow 'Olympic' triathlon a few months earlier, I told myself, 'You only have to do this three more times'. Just two 70.3s and an Ironman and I could stop messing around and go back to just doing the running thing. So I had booked my place at The Gauntlet, signed up for Ironman UK and found another half-iron triathlon to do in the build-up to it. I completed The Gauntlet, however shakily, and started 2014 with just those final two triathlons in my calendar. Two more and I could stop.

A year after I'd made myself that promise in Marlow at my first ever standard distance tri, something strange happened. I wanted to pull on my tri suit, grab my bike and do it all again. I'd enjoyed running, cycling and swimming for a while now, but doing all three in quick succession was something that didn't necessarily fill me with excitement. As I began training for the Ironman, I realised how much I'd underestimated that first sprint distance race and how unprepared I was for that and my Olympic distance race. And I wanted to go back and do them again, one year on – now a more confident swimmer and stronger on the bike – just a bit better. I wasn't concerned about my finish time or position; I was fine with being right at the back of the pack. And while I knew that with a year's extra training I'd probably do better the next time around, that wasn't the main motivation or goal. I wanted to do another standard distance triathlon to enjoy it, and to feel comfortable, instead of it being another stage to tick off between me and my ultimate goal in Bolton. I wanted to enjoy a triathlon.

As if by magic, that spring an offer came along to take part in the Olympic distance race at the World Triathlon in London in June. The start was just a 5-mile downhill cycle from my front door, which would make a change from cramming my bike onto a train or into the back of a taxi. It was in Hyde Park, a place I've run round many times training for marathons and there'd be no traffic on the bike course because the roads were closed. Best of all, there'd be waved starts that went on throughout the day so, even if I was the slowest cyclist in the race, I'd still have company during the bike leg. So I said yes, and I asked Katie to join me. Of course she said yes too.

The race is part of the ITU World Triathlon Series where the best athletes in the world battle it out. They raced on the Saturday and on the Sunday there's an open event for anyone to enter with standard, sprint and super sprint distance options. Katie and I headed to Hyde Park on the Saturday to watch the pros racing, to get excited, and to pick up our race packs. After a couple of hours watching the Brownlees race past us as we sat in the grandstand, sweating in jeans, we thought it would be a good idea to get out of the sun and start the prep for our own race. We headed off to the pub to eat pizza and drink beer that came from Kona, Hawaii, home of the Ironman World Championships, in the hope that it would bring us some luck.

The next morning, we cycled through London in our tri suits carrying our wetsuits and some snacks on our backs, ready to be at the start for 10.10 a.m. We lined up on the pontoon where we'd watched the Brownlees dive into the Serpentine from the day before. Katie headed to the middle ready to fight it out with the speedy swimmers while I hung back and tried to grab a spot at the side. Unlike the pros, we weren't allowed to dive in so we all plopped into the water rather ungracefully and were asked to hold onto the side until the horn signalled for our wave to start.

As the horn sounded, I counted to ten and waited for the splashing to move away from me before starting to swim. Waves set off every 10 minutes and I was concerned I might get run over by the speedy swimmers of the wave behind. But then there were a pair of feet in front of my goggles, and then another. I'd caught up with the pack.

Although my main goal was to enjoy the race, I hoped that with a year's more experience, I might get a swim PB. I didn't want to swim in the pack, but I didn't want to slow down either. So I had no option but to get stuck in and carry on swimming. The swim course was a 1,500 m rectangular lap. I made it to the first two corners and as I swam round the buoys I glanced back and saw a couple of swimmers behind me. It was a long straight swim to the other end of the rectangle. There were pairs of feet in front of me and swimmers on either side. As I lifted my head to the side to breathe, there was the face of another swimmer staring back at me doing the same. I swam over a green swim cap lying on the bottom of the lake and I wondered what had happened to its owner.

I swam round the last two buoys and back towards the pontoon and then I was running up the exit ramp, this time with other swimmers around me. I knew I'd swum faster than last time. I ran towards transition, past the cheering squad from my running club, Serpentine RC, and I gave them a thumbs-up that it was going OK.

I jumped on my bike ready for five laps of a course that took us in a C-shape, with two hairpin turns at either end. There were speed bumps, there were sharp turns, and there was a small bit of gradient to keep it interesting. There were also lots of other cyclists around from the different waves. It made a nice change to cycle with other triathletes, even though most of them were overtaking me.

I saw Katie going in the opposite direction, and then cycling past me asking if I had any fig rolls. And then I didn't see her again and knew she'd finished and was already onto the run. By the fifth lap, the course was familiar, which made the turns, the (small) climbs and the (marginal) descents much quicker. I had a speedometer on my bike and knew I was quicker than in Marlow a year before, but didn't know by how much.

Then came the run: four laps of the Serpentine. It was nice to be off the bike. For the first few steps anyway. Then my legs complained. My hips complained. My calves complained. But I'd been here before, I knew I'd feel better after the first lap was over. And I did. Marginally.

I was cheered on after every lap by the Serpentine cheering squad. I wasn't wearing club colours but they recognised me as one of their own and gave me a big shout. The laps ticked by, running past the finishing line three times, before being able to turn left on the blue carpet and attempt a sprint finish.

Katie was waiting at the finishing line as I collected my medal. We'd both had a good race. I could tell from the clock that I'd get a PB. But because the clock was showing the time of day, rather than race time, I didn't know exactly how much I'd taken off last year's time. It wasn't until I got home and checked the results that I would find out. My swim time was 32.22, a whole 11 minutes faster than a year before. The bike took 1.23.20 and the run 50.11 with my overall time being 2.55.47, a 37 minute PB. But what mattered most was that I'd improved on last year's race in other ways: I hadn't been scared of the swim, I hadn't had to stop during it, I'd smiled through the bike, and I'd decided that Bolton wouldn't be the end of my triathlons. I'd started to enjoy triathlon – which was lucky because I had another one to do in exactly a week's time.

'Why does it have to be so early?' asked my friend Helen again.

When she'd agreed to put me up the night before my half-iron race and then drive me to the start, she had forgotten how triathletes like to get the party started very early. I woke her up at 6.30 a.m. and we were out the door in minutes, hurtling down the motorway for the 7.30 start. The sun had already been up for hours and it was starting to get warm.

The Grafman half-iron distance race near St Neots was my first introduction to two things: a 'beach start', where swimmers start on dry land and run into the water, and an 'Australian exit'. An Australian exit, despite sounding like the latest bikini waxing fad, just means you have to get out the water and run round a marker before getting back in and swimming a second lap.

I stood on the 'beach' of Grafham Water reservoir and watched the first two waves swimming their first lap. Then a horn sounded and my wave charged towards the water, none of us managing to do it with the *Baywatch*-esque grace that we'd envisioned. There were more swimmers around me than in the triathlon the week before, but I tried to relax and not panic.

As we turned back towards the shore for the end of the first lap, the fast men from the first wave began overtaking me. 'Don't panic, they know what they're doing,' I reassured myself and they passed by without too much fuss.

As I staggered out of the water for the Australian exit, I could hear my mum, who'd arrived with my dad just after the start, shouting out. I waved and then staggered back into the water for the second lap. Getting out, standing up and seeing the spectators made my heart rate rise and I had to calm myself down again and relax for the second half. Ironman UK in Bolton has a similar mid-swim exit, so this was good practice.

My sighting became a bit rubbish midway through both laps and I swam slightly off course but, before long, I was turning back to the exit and running out the water. The swim was over, I ran the short distance to my bike, waved to my dad, and smiled as the announcer said my name three times because he was getting such a big cheer from my small band of spectators.

I'd looked at the 2013 results for this race a few days before. 'I'm going to be last off the bike again.'

'I think it's very cool that you no longer say this about the swim,' was Katie's reply.

I sat on the grass putting on my socks and bike shoes in transition as people were still coming in from the water. It was quite cool to think how far I'd come.

Out on the bike course, those same people were soon overtaking me, but I was OK with that. The route took us on a small loop before heading past the start to a bigger out and back loop that we'd do twice. Despite being at the back, there was always someone going the opposite direction to smile at, or faster cyclists on their second lap speeding past to entertain me. The marshals were the friendliest and most enthusiastic I'd seen in a long time, and the roads were quiet.

I looked up at the sky; it was bright blue with a few bright white clouds floating across it. It looked like it had been painted. Whenever I wanted the cycle to be over, I tried to think that there probably wasn't anywhere better to be than on a bike right now.

After about 40 miles, I got off my bike and bent down next to it, looking at the wheel. A woman slowed down as she went past and asked if I was OK. 'Yes, fine thanks.' Then a man who was just behind her stopped and asked what was wrong. 'I'm fine really.'

'Do you need some help?'

'No, I'm OK.'

'Are you sure? Is it... ?'

'Actually, I'm having a wee.'

'Oh, sorry.'

He pedalled off and I realised he was the back marker. I was now the last rider. I jumped back on my bike and, as I pedalled past him, he followed behind me, keeping his distance. I pedalled hard to overtake the rider in front of me, partly through pride and partly through embarrassment. I caught her after about 6 miles and then had just 10 miles to make sure she didn't catch me. 'Stretching!' I thought, 'I should have said I was stretching.'

As I turned into transition to cheers from my spectators, I looked back: there were just a couple of hundred metres between us.

As I racked my bike, an official came over to check on me. 'Are you feeling OK? Are you well enough to start the run?'

'Yes, this is the bit I like!'

'Good to hear. Off you go!'

The two-lap run took us on two out and back sections that meant going past the transition and finish area three times.

This would prove very handy for me. Half a mile into the run I realised I didn't have my number on – I must have taken it off by mistake when I got off the bike. I'd be disqualified if I crossed the finishing line like this. Should I run back into transition, mess up the timing chip and risk a disqualification for re-entering transition? I kept running. By the time I'd turned and headed back towards my support crew, I'd formed a plan. I stopped where they were waiting, there was another number in the bag they had. After some fumbling, I was off again holding my number in my hand. The second time I came past them, they'd managed to get some safety pins. As I started the second lap with my number pinned to my front, my legs started to feel much better and I started speeding up.

Each time I overtook another runner it gave me a burst of energy to keep going. I was feeling pretty good and starting to enjoy the run. In the last mile, I overtook a group of four men. One of them would come up to me after the finish to congratulate me on my sprint finish and tell me he hated me as I ran past. I ran as fast as my legs would go towards the finishing line and finished the race smiling.

When I'd signed up for The Grafman six months earlier, I'd looked at the cut-off times for each stage. The bike leg had to be completed 5.5 hours after the start of the race, including the time taken for the swim – I was worried I wouldn't make it. But I made the cut-offs with time to spare and finished The Grafman in 6.36.34. I'd hoped to finish the bike leg in less than 4 hours and in the end I did it in 3 hours 45 minutes. I was pretty happy about this. More importantly though, unlike my first 70.3, there were no tears for this half-iron triathlon. Only smiles.

KATIE

'No socks, please. We're triathletes': The dark art of transition

With three sports in one morning, you're going to have to get changed twice during this race. Known as 'transition', this is often called the fourth discipline and triathletes can take this astonishingly seriously. When asked if I should put socks on in my first sprint triathlon, my experienced triathlete friend, Rachel, replied, 'Katie, you may as well take your hair straighteners.' However, I was recently asked by another friend whether I wear my wetsuit when I cycle, so I think this is probably one area of the sport where most people have questions as they prepare for their first race. There is no need to feel alone, we'll run through each step here. And if you want to wear socks, you can (though perhaps not for the swim).

What is transition?

Transition is the change of kit between each of the three sports; since the clock starts at the beginning of the swim, and stops at the end of your run, the time taken to do this is counted in your total time and is why it can become the obsession of many a triathlete.

At your triathlon, there will be a transition area, where your bike and kit are stored, and where you change between kit. Since there will be two changes during the race, transition is often referred to as T1 (transition 1 from swim to bike) and T2 (transition from bike to run). In the transition area, there will be racking for bikes, normally fashioned from long horizontal scaffolding poles, held up above saddle height so that bikes can hang by the saddle or handlebars; and a small area on the ground for each participant to store kit. At busy events, space can be at a premium in transition, so don't be surprised if you feel like your bike and kit are squashed up to the next competitor; however, do respect the space of those around you and try to avoid spreading out your stuff too far.

Since you'll be leaving your bike there, transition areas are patrolled by marshals to ensure security and you will normally need to show your race number to gain access; the same applies after the race to collect your bike. At some races, T1 and T2 are in separate locations and there will be two transition areas; this will mean that you leave your bike and cycling kit in T1, and your running kit in T2, where the cycle would also finish and your bike can be racked. Transition areas can get busy during a race so there will be a clear entry point from the swim into T1 and normally a different exit on to the bike course. Likewise, there will be a bike entry point and run exit once you have completed T2. It's always worth spending a little time before your race working out where each of these is located. You may not be too worried how long your transition takes for your first race, but you'll wish you'd checked when you

<label>192</label>

inadvertently extend your run by circling transition looking for a way out.

The naked truth

If, at this stage, the idea of all this public changing of kit all sounds a bit exhibitionistic, don't worry: triathlon is the only sport I know where they feel the need to actively prohibit nipple exposure (the British Triathlon rules state 'the minimum is a one- or two-piece non-transparent swimsuit' and that the upper body and 'especially the chest area' should be firmly under wraps during the cycle and run). Tri suits are a popular choice, and offer slightly more dignity than having to run in a swimming costume. A tri suit is, essentially, a vest and shorts stitched together, a little like a tight version of a Victorian bathing suit, with a padded chamois section in the shorts for the comfort of your undercarriage on the bike. You don't need to spend a fortune on one either; I picked up my first tri suit from a famous German discount supermarket chain for £10 about five years ago and it's still going strong, so keep your eyes peeled for offers.

As you already know, I was put off getting into triathlon at first as an adult, not because I was worried about the three sports, but because I couldn't understand how I was going to run without a sports bra, or put one on after swimming. Then Rachel gave me a simple solution: wear one. A comfortable sports bra under your tri suit can be worn throughout the race, including the swim, and will save you a visit from the Nipple Police. If you don't want to invest in a tri suit at first, then a pair of shorts that you're happy to swim, cycle and run in could be an option, with a sports bra on top for the girls, and a T-shirt thrown over after the swim. Aside from the modesty issues, if you can wear the same thing to swim, cycle and run, even as just a base layer, then you'll minimise the changing and therefore the time taken in transition.

Swim to bike: T1

Whether there are one or two transition areas, T1 will be somewhere near the swim exit, either from a pool or open water. At some races, you can expect to run a short distance, or up to a few hundred metres to your transition; this is more common with open-water races than pool swims but it can be a good opportunity to wake up the legs before the cycle. Don't worry, you won't get bored: there's plenty to be getting on with, especially if you have a wetsuit to take off.

In a pool swim, check where the exit door is in relation to the pool so that you can jump straight out and get going to the transition area. If you're swimming in open water, use the last 100 m to sight where the swim exit is; this will save you having to bob around and slow down as you close in towards the end. Kicking your legs a bit harder in the last few metres can help to wake them up a little before they take centre stage for the rest of the race. Swim as close as you can to the exit, pushing yourself up to your feet with your arms when the water becomes too shallow. If you're exiting from deeper water, there will normally be marshals to help pull you from the water – stick out your arm, listen to their instructions and embrace the help. Take a second to get your balance if you need to (as you go from horizontal to vertical, you can feel a little wobbly but it will pass) and get running.

Removing a wetsuit becomes more difficult the drier it gets so, before you leave the water, tug gently at the neck and let some water flow in; this will create a layer of water between you and the wetsuit so you can escape like an easy-peel satsuma. Put your goggles up onto your forehead, reach behind for the zip cord and unzip the back of the suit as soon as you're out of the water. Take your arms out of the sleeves and roll it down to your waist as soon as you can; you can do this while running towards T1 as it will save time, and prevent it drying out before you've had chance to take it off. Take off your hat and goggles and, when you get to your bike, pull the whole suit down to your ankles, and use one foot at a time to stand on the suit and free the other foot. It's just another aspect of triathlon that scores low marks in the elegance category.

Finding your bike can be tricky among all the others in transition, but the straight rows of racks mean that you can count them off. When you're racking your bike before the race, always spend a few moments working out how you will remember where your bike is. If you're still a bit wobbly from the swim, or the cold water has given you an ice cream headache, you won't want to be running up and down trying to find your stuff.

Place your hat, goggles, and wetsuit neatly on the floor next to your bike, if you tuck them under the raised end of your bike (the back wheel will be up in the air if you rack the bike by the saddle, or the front if hanging by the handlebars) then it will stop your wetsuit getting in yours or anyone else's way. Spreading your kit out messily and hindering others can result in a time penalty; it's triathlon equivalent of losing your pocket money for not tidying your room. If this sounds petty, then it's worth remembering that you're less likely to lose your stuff if you're tidy.

Now that it's time to get changed, remember that you've got your basic gear on already, be that a tri suit or shorts.

Boys, if it's the latter, then remember to put a top on now and keep those nipplephobes happy. Depending on the length of your race, or the temperature, you may want to put on a top for the cycle anyway. I tend to put a cycling jersey on for a standard distance or longer, mainly because I can put some food in the pockets, but plenty of people ride and run in just their tri suits. If you're using a race belt for your race number, put this on with the number on your back for the cycle. Time to honk the triathlon rule hooter again! Cycle helmets are compulsory for the bike section in triathlon and must be put on and fastened before you can move your bike from the rack; to ensure you don't forget this, put on your cycle helmet and fasten it immediately.

Leaving a small towel on the floor in your transition space will mean that you can stand on it and dry off your feet a little, and wipe off any dirt or grass picked up running from the swim (a bit of grit in your shoes will bug you like a bee in your bike helmet). If you're opting for socks, roll down the tops to put them on, then step into your shoes. Wearing your running shoes is fine on the bike and it will save you a few moments in T2 if you're doing your first triathlon or haven't been cycling long; however, if you plan to do any more cycling or triathlon, then you will probably want to move on to cycling shoes that clip into the pedals.

There are two main options for putting on cycling shoes in T1: the first is easiest, where you put them on as you would trainers and run out of transition wearing them; the second involves a particular form of advanced triathlon voodoo where you clip your shoes to your pedals before the race, run out of transition barefoot, and put your feet into the shoes once you have hopped onto the bike. To keep the shoes upright and in a horizontal position, competitors fashion some extraordinary elastic band attachments between the shoe, cranks, and parts of the frame, which snap as you pedal away. Done well, it is faster than putting on your shoes in transition but it involves a lot of skill and it takes plenty of practice, not to mention sharp wits and confidence riding one-handed as you do up the Velcro straps on the move, so it's best left until you've cut your teeth on your first few races. I've tried it a few times but haven't done so since a race where the bike course went almost immediately up a hill and my feet were left floating above the pedals, without the speed to freewheel for a moment and sort out the shoes. Instead, I tend to opt for trotting through transition in my cycling shoes like a goat on cobbles.

Once ready, lift the bike slightly from the rack to unhook it and push it away towards the bike exit. Do not be tempted to jump on the bike now. Riding in transition is not allowed, mainly for safety reasons; instead, there will be a line drawn after the bike exit, called the 'mount line', and once the bike is completely past this point, you will be allowed to pedal away. As you become more practised, pushing it along by the saddle makes it easier to steer as you run out of transition, and it saves you the agony of getting knocked in the back of your ankle by your pedals, but if you feel safer pushing along by the handlebars, do that. In all the excitement, the point where everyone jumps on their bike can be a little chaotic; the most important thing is to be alert and safe. If you're at all nervous, move to one side and take a moment to get onto your bike safely, taking a look around you before you pedal away. You may see people leaping energetically onto their bikes at speed, but that speed means nothing if they end up in a hedge.

Congratulations! You are safely through T1 and on the bike leg of the triathlon.

T1 summary:

- Locate the swim exit.

- Let a little water into your wetsuit before you leave the water.

- Remove the top of your wetsuit on the way to your bike.

- Locate your bike in transition.

- Take your legs out of the wetsuit at your bike.

- Fasten your race belt with the number on your back.

- Put on your helmet and fasten the straps.

- Quick dry your feet, put on shoes.

- Unrack your bike and push it out of the cycle exit.

- Get on your bike once it is completely past the mount line.

Bike to run: T2

With the cycle nearly complete, you just have the run left to go. If you have yet to experience this, running straight after a bike ride is an extraordinary feeling and it can take a bit of getting used to at first. You can help ease the changeover by selecting a lower gear for the last 5 minutes or so on your bike; spinning in this gear will help your legs feel a little more spritely and prepare them to turnover at a higher cadence when you're running.

Just as there was a mount line after T1, there is a dismount line before T2, which will be clearly marked and marshalled before the transition area. Unlike a dismount in gymnastics, this is not the icing on the cake of your routine and no amount of flourish will score you extra points; instead, slow down with sufficient time to be able to unclip your cycling shoes and get off your bike before the line. Again, you will see others doing this at speed but, having just pedalled as hard as you can, this is a part of the course where people are tired and mistakes can easily be made. Keep your wits about you, look around as you slow down, and draw to a speed where you feel confident getting off your bike safely. Then push your bike into transition, running, if you can, to continue getting your legs ready for the next stage.

Normally, T2 will be in the same location as T1, in which case you will rack your bike in the same place as before. If there is a separate T2, you will have already placed your running kit in your space and you will rack your bike there. Either way, it's important to know where your space is: without your bike there, you will only really have your trainers as a marker so you will make life easier for yourself by remembering their approximate location. Rack your bike by the handlebars or saddle, just as you did before the race in T1. Only when your bike is racked can you unclip your helmet strap and take off your bike helmet; again, failure to do this can result in a time penalty.

If you wore trainers to cycle, you're pretty much ready to go; if you wore cycling shoes then step out of each shoe and into your trainers. Turn your race belt to face the front and charge out of the run exit. Of course, you will have left your transition space neat and tidy, to keep the triathlon gods happy but, no matter how organised you've been, as you begin your run, you will still feel like you've left two vital pieces of equipment behind: your legs. Keep going, the feeling will ease and you can pat yourself of the back that you've made it onto the final stage of your triathlon.

T2 summary:

- Change into a lower gear for the last 5 minutes of the cycle.

- Slow down and get off your bike before the dismount line.

- Push your bike into transition, run if you can.

- Locate your racking space.

- Rack your bike by the saddle or handlebars.

- Remove your cycle helmet.

- Change into running trainers.

- Check any removed cycling kit is left neatly in your area.

- Turn your race number to the front.

- Run out of transition via the run exit.

Getting set up in transition before your race

- You'll have to carry some kit and push your bike into T1 to get set up. Carry your cycling shoes, running shoes, race belt, helmet in a small bag (a carrier bag will do) so that you don't drop anything on the way. Some people use plastic boxes but they can be tricky to handle with your bike. Family, supporters, colleagues or pets are not allowed into the transition area with you so you'll need to be able to manage your kit by yourself.

- Ensure that you have the race numbers, which may include a 'paper' number and some stickers for your bike and/or helmet, and attach them according to the instructions given by the race organiser. Your race number could be attached to a top but, since most events require the number to be displayed on the back for the cycle and front for the run, a race belt (a thick piece of elasticated fabric to which a number can be pinned) is a good option; this becomes essential if the race organiser has only issued one number. You won't need to wear your paper number to swim.

- There will normally be a quick safety check on your bike before you enter the transition area; this is to ensure that your bike is roadworthy and the main checks will be that your brakes work and that the handlebars are covered at the ends (road bike handlebars have bar end plugs; flat handlebars normally have rubber grips that do this). At this point, the marshal may ask you to put on your cycle helmet and fasten the strap; this is not because there is stuff falling from the sky in the transition but just to check that you have a helmet and that it fastens securely.

- Ensure that your tyres are inflated before your race. If you are asked to rack your bike on race morning, check the tyres before you go to the transition area. Some races with particularly early starts might ask you to rack your bike the night before, so you should go and check the tyres again in the morning. If you're racking the night before and it's particularly hot, it's sensible to let a little air out and re-inflate the morning after, so that pressure changes caused by the heat don't cause an inner tube to burst.

● Put your bike into a gear suitable for the start of the bike course. More often than not, a lower gear is better as it will allow you to get your legs moving easily before changing up; this is particularly important if there is a hill shortly after the start.

● Check where you are allowed to rack your bike. Some races will designate space according to your race number; some allow a free-for-all. If you are allowed to choose, there is some advantage in racking closer to the end of a row so that your stuff is easier to locate; others will be looking to do this so if it's not possible, spend a few moments working out some landmarks to help you to locate your space during the race. You wouldn't leave your car in a multi-storey car park before checking how you're going to find it later. Counting the number of racks and working out approximately how far along you are from the end of the rack is the simplest way to do this; there may also be signs in transition that can provide additional cues. Avoid using other people's bikes or kit as markers, since they may not be there when you are in transition. While it seems a good idea, you're not supposed to place any markers on your bike that would give you an advantage in finding it so perhaps consider making your next running shoe purchase a particularly garish pair.

● Rack your bike according to the marshals' instructions: you can either hang the bike by hooking the handlebars or the front of your saddle onto the rack. If you have a choice then by the saddle is generally better as it's narrower and less likely to get in a tangle than the handlebars, and your bike will be facing forwards to wheel it out of T1. Generally, it makes sense to rack on alternate sides of the bar with the people next to you; if in doubt, always ask a marshal.

* Place your cycle helmet upside down on the handlebars, if it will balance; but if it's windy, or it seems a bit precarious, place the helmet on the floor next to your bike.

* A folded towel on the floor is handy to quickly dry your feet on and you can place your race belt, cycling shoes and/or running shoes on it so that they are ready for you. If you are going to wear socks, place one in each shoe so that they are ready to be put on.

* Leave your cycling shoes undone so that you can put them on quickly. Putting running trainers on quickly can be made easier with lace locks (a little plastic widget like the ones you get on a rucksack drawstring) or elastic laces, or simply by leaving them untied. I've mistakenly left mine in a double knot before now and it's the sort of thing you only do once. Many people sprinkle a bit of talc into the heels of their shoes to help put them on; try it at home first and see if it helps you.

* Keep it neat. Remember that your kit must be arranged so that it doesn't impede anyone else's space. How you position your kit exactly becomes a very personal preference over time but, whatever you choose, transition is no place for a 'walk-on' wardrobe.

* If T1 and T2 are in separate locations, place your cycle helmet and cycling shoes with your bike in T1. In T2, place your trainers (if you haven't worn them to cycle) on a little towel in your racking space, where your bike will go after the cycle.

- Find out where the swim entrance, bike exit, bike entrance and run exit are all located with respect to your transition spot and have a think about which way you will run to and from your bike. You could also have a look where the mount and dismount lines are so that you can picture what you're going to have to do.

- Get your swimming gear together and get ready to go! You are ready for your triathlon!

It might seem like a lot to take on board at first and the idea of learning to get changed quickly may even seem a funny way to save time in a sporting event. The more races you do, the more you will get used to what works for you, and learn where savings can be made. Transition is certainly worth giving some thought to: in the simplest sense this can just involve working out what you're going to wear and what order you're going to wear it in so that you're calm on race day. More dedicated transition preparation can involve practising the changes in training, and the skills such as the bike mount and dismount. I've even seen someone miming the whole process, which included the adornment and fastening of an invisible air helmet, in transition on the morning of a race. If this all still sounds a bit silly, think how hard you'd have to train to knock a minute off your 5 km run PB; then think how long it took to put on a pair of leggings or tight jeans after your last swim at the pool and how much time and effort you'd have saved if only you'd given that one some more thought beforehand.

LAURA

Ruled with a rod of iron: Training for Bolton

Summer was finally here. After months of running in the cold of winter, and spinning away on the turbo to avoid the downpours of spring, finally the sun was out, the water in lidos and lakes was warming up and training was becoming a joy.

On one of the nicest days we'd had so far, a Friday when the sun was shining but not too hot, the sky was blue and the grass dry, I curled up on my bed and cried. I didn't know why I was crying and I didn't know how to stop. It had started because I was hungry, which led to an argument about being late for dinner. It started hours before that as I'd cycled home and was almost knocked off my bike by another cyclist looking at their phone instead of the road. He laughed at me when I told him to look where he was going and I shouted down the road at him in anger. It started before that when a driver had wound down her window and told me to signal where I was going: I was going straight ahead and I didn't know the appropriate hand signal for that. It started with a 6 a.m. start to do a turbo session on the bike before meeting a coach to discuss the last four weeks of my Ironman training. It started with realising the enormity of what I had to do and facing a weekend of more 6 a.m. starts to do the longest bike and swim of my training so far. The past 26 weeks had flown by too fast. I wanted to blow a whistle, call a time out and have a week off to catch my breath and catch up on sleep. But that wasn't going to happen.

Training for the Ironman had also been a lot of fun and a lot more manageable than I ever expected it to be. But it wasn't exclusively fun for 30 weeks. The juggling of two swim sessions, a couple of runs a week, plus a few cycles and a long ride at the weekend was challenging in many ways. As well as pushing my physical limits, I had to find creative ways to fit them all into a seven day period while still going to work, seeing friends occasionally, washing my kit and feeding myself.

One Monday evening, I collapsed onto the sofa, exhausted from a weekend of training and a day at work. In the kitchen, the dishes were stacked up waiting for me to wash them and a pile of dirty sports gear sat in the hallway of my tiny flat, ready for me to move it a few metres to the washing machine. But it would all have to wait. I was already tending to another more pressing matter: treating the verruca on my foot.

This isn't the glamorous, inspiring side of training for a triathlon. It wasn't fun. Nobody would want to take a picture of this scene and post it to Instagram, but it was just as much a part of the training as the sunny bike rides that I had taken photos of. Keeping normal life ticking along and keeping on top of the administrative tasks, keeping yourself fed and watered, and making sure you have a clean pair of knickers for work tomorrow: it all takes a huge amount of effort when all you want to do is sit down on the sofa and do nothing.

Eventually I did stop crying on that Friday evening. I washed my face and I went out for some dinner. I returned home an hour later with a belly full of Thai food and went to bed, ready to be up early the next morning to swim. It was the biggest weekend of training I'd done so far and there were only three weekends left.

The next morning I arrived at Parliament Hill Lido at 7.30 a.m. ready to swim 3 km. This would be the furthest I'd ever swum. And, because Stoke Newington Reservoir, my usual open-water swimming spot, was closed due to algae, I'd be doing it in a pool. My heart sank as I had read a tweet a couple of days earlier announcing that the reservoir was closed to all activities.

Through the weeks of winter training in the pool, I'd found myself looking forward to the start of the open-water swim season. Clocking up the distance in the pool had become a chore. Each time I pushed off the wall at the end of the lane, having to swim round another swimmer or having another overtake me a little too closely splashing water into my mouth, I thought about swimming in the lake. These things didn't happen in the lake. It was a complete change from the nervous swimmer who'd gone swimming in a gale that evening last May. Katie had told me that once I got used to swimming in open water, I'd realise how much better it was than following the black tile line on the bottom of a pool. 'It's like running outside compared to running on the treadmill.' Like many things, she was right about this too.

Most weekends since the London Marathon in April, I'd been up early on a Saturday or Sunday morning to do laps of the reservoir. That first weekend, the water was cold and it took me a good 5 minutes to get in. Getting into the cold water is the worst part of swimming outside but week by week the water got warmer and the time it took for me to warm up and calm down got shorter. Lowering myself into the water and swimming round the orange marker buoys pretty much undisturbed by anyone for an hour was one of my favourite parts of the week. That was until the week when I'd planned to swim my furthest distance yet. That was the week that the reservoir was closed.

I wasn't excited about swimming 3 km in a lido. It was forecast to be 24°C that weekend and lidos get pretty busy when the sun comes out. I met up with my friend, Josie, another refugee from Stoke Newington Reservoir, in the changing rooms. We'd decided that it would be more fun to swim laps together, and I had a lot of laps to do: it would take 50 laps of the 60-metre pool to reach 3,000 metres.

I swam up and down and stopped halfway through to speak to Josie.

'A man just swam over the top of me, it was quite impressive really,' she told me.

It was busy. There was only one lane roped off in the pool and a local triathlon squad was using it. We swam in the remainder of the pool with everyone else who was doing laps of various styles and speeds. There was no system to it and every so often I'd swim towards a wall of swimmers, three people wide, approaching from the other end of the pool. After a few goes, I found the best way to deal with this was to keep swimming and eventually a gap would appear in the wall for me to swim through.

The Parliament Hill Lido has an unusual metal liner to it. Apparently, it's the only outdoor pool in the country with a liner of this kind. On sunny days, the sun reflects off the metal and makes the water sparkle under the surface. In the stretches of clear water, when I didn't have to avoid other swimmers, there was something very magical about swimming there.

As I clocked up 1,900 metres in the pool, I was into uncharted territory – this was the furthest I'd swum before. I carried on feeling good and relaxed. A few lengths later, I could smell something. The cafe at the side of the pool was open for business and serving up breakfasts. I could smell toast wafting across the water and I was getting hungry.

Josie finished her session before I did and sat on the side cheering and counting down my laps for me. 'Four more to go... Two more to go... ' As I approached 3,000 metres, I'd begun to feel cold. The water was warm – warmer than the reservoir and I hadn't felt cold there in weeks. I carried on and Josie gave me a cheer as I touched the wall at the end of my final lap. I got out the pool and water fell out the ankles of my suit.

'I don't think that's supposed to happen,' said Josie.

I lifted up my arm where three big holes had appeared in my suit. I'd learnt a lot of things in the past six months, next up was how to repair a wetsuit, it seemed.

In the afternoon, I caught the train up to my parents' home in Peterborough, ready for a 74-mile cycle sportive and my sister's birthday on the Sunday. 'I've got a hen party to go to tonight so your dad's cooking,' said my mum. He cooks a mean curry aided solely by the telephone and a takeaway menu. I went to bed early, full of food. The next morning, I stopped 30 miles into my ride to eat sandwiches made by my mum, realising that it was only 9.30 a.m., and I'd already been riding for 2 hours. I was doing the 'Flat Out in the Fens' sportive along with Phil, who had a shiny new road bike that I know he wanted to storm ahead, but he kindly stayed with me the whole way.

Over the past couple of months, as my swimming had got better and I had started to realise quite how far the bike leg of an Ironman was, the cycle became my area of concern. One hundred and twelve miles, 1,270 metres of climbing: I could recall these numbers easier than my PIN number.

'Try not to get too hung up on the profile. It's not going to change. Just get out on some hills!' This was Katie's very sensible advice. So that's what I did. Two weeks after running the London Marathon, I cycled from London to Cambridge, conveniently a half-iron cycle distance, to meet my parents for a pub crawl. I cycled up 427 m of climb. It wasn't easy, but it was easier than it used to be. I spent a rainy Saturday with four other women cycling from London to Brighton. The route was around 60 miles and involved some pretty big hills. We cycled, we ate crisps and cake, we got rained on, we sweated, we got blown around on our bikes by strong gusts of wind and we smiled a lot. Above all else, we had fun and we encouraged each other. I cycled 90 miles to Peterborough, stopping off at St Neots overnight, 60 miles into the journey, and cycling on the rest of the way the next morning. I cycled around Surrey and up Box Hill with my friend, Jason – it was easier than the year before when I'd cycled up it as part of Ride London 100 and I wondered whether this was because I'd got better or because I hadn't cycled 70 miles to get here this time. I cycled up Swains Lane, a hill in North London, five times in a row, a total of 387 metres of climbing.

I followed pink signs around the Fens for more than 5 hours, never getting lost and chatting with Phil about how much our bums hurt and whether local anaesthetic is a viable option for cyclists. We arrived back at my sister's house where my running shoes were waiting for me to do one last mile round the block on foot as per the instructions I'd been given by my new coach, Chris, on that Friday before the floods of tears. I stumbled back in the gate 8 minutes later, in time for my sister's birthday barbeque to start. Gradually, distances that had once seemed daunting were exciting because they were taking me to new places.

I did what I could to prepare for Bolton but I wasn't doing it alone. From Josie swimming with me at the lido, Phil keeping me company on the bike, my dad making dinner, my mum packing me a sandwich, and my sister timing her birthday barbeque to coincide with the finish of my cycle, there were lots of people helping me along the way. Training for an Ironman wasn't something that isolated me from people, it was quite the opposite.

Training was a lot of fun but, when I thought about what it was all building towards, it sometimes overwhelmed me. It kept me up at night, it made me obsess over the stats of each bike ride I did rather than how much I'd enjoyed it, and it had me crying my eyes out on a Friday night four weeks before the race.

 **KATIE**

Goggle marks and early starts:
Tips to achieve the training–life balance

Contrary to what you may hear, training for three sports does not have to mean training three times as hard. Pacing isn't just an important part of getting through an endurance event on the day, it's also important when it comes to your training. When planning your build-up to a triathlon, it's important to keep in perspective the amount of training you can realistically fit in, while keeping the plates spinning in your day-to-day life. That said, there are a number of ways that you can make the most of the time that you have available and, with some resourceful time management, you can become a master of the triathlon training-life balance.

Value added

You've downloaded a plan from the Internet, printed it, read it, and now you've just gone and spat your cup of tea all over it.

Why? You've realised quite how many sessions you're expected to squeeze in each week. Don't panic: remember that one plan will not fit all and it's important that you consider where your strengths and weaknesses are. If you're going to trim any sessions, make sure you do leave in the ones that will focus on your weaker area. If you're a runner, trust that your legs will remember how to do this, even if you cut down your number of weekly run sessions, and benefit instead from more time invested in swimming and cycling. Triathlon requires balance between the three sports so you can't afford to neglect any of the disciplines completely but, if you're strapped for time, focusing on your weaker areas will give the most value added for time invested.

Embrace the variety

'Don't cry that you have three sports to train for, smile that you don't have to go cycling in the rain…' is what Dr Seuss would have said, if he had been preparing for his first triathlon. Training for three sports has some real advantages: the combination of swimming, cycling and running can give your body a bit of a break from the pressures of just one sport; the variety can be a real positive when it comes to maintaining interest and commitment in your training programme; and, if it's pouring with rain and a bike ride doesn't appeal, the chances are the pool is open and you can shift your sessions around a little that week. There's never an excuse not to get your hair wet.

Hit the road

A change of scene can be just the ticket to combine your training with a spot of travelling. If you want to make your training the focus of your trip, then there are training camps held in all sorts of lovely locations. The training resort, Club La Santa, in Lanzarote and the mountains on the island of Mallorca are examples of renowned European hubs for cycling and triathlon training trips; both offer the opportunity to train your heart out in the daytime, and recover in the sun afterwards.

If you're looking for an active holiday but prefer not to think of it as training, you could consider something a bit more adventurous and explore somewhere new by swimming, cycling or running. I have a friend who cycled between vineyards in France in the run-up to her iron-distance triathlon, and there are companies, such as SwimTrek, who will take you wild swimming in some beautiful places. Of course, a more 'normal' holiday doesn't mean that you need to pack up your training completely. Take your trainers or hire a bike to explore a new city under your own steam, and pack your swimming kit to practise a few skills in the hotel pool or go for a swim in a bay. Remember to be realistic though: you're unlikely to fit in a full week of training, especially if you're travelling with friends and family who aren't in training for a triathlon, so keep active but enjoy the break so you come back fresh to your training when you return.

It's all very well heading off to the Med for a couple of weeks of rain-free training during the winter months, but if you're on more of a budget, then you can always look a bit closer to home. Laura has been known to transform her flat into a base for her exclusive London-based triathlon training camp, 'Club La Banter', kindly hosting me for a weekend of lido swimming, spin class cycling, and running a 10 km race; there was also a bit of practice in the fourth and fifth disciplines, namely getting changed a lot and celebrating with curry and beer. Don't worry, Laura had it all planned out, 'Some may look on this as foolish but the wise know this to be an essential training technique; fear of toilet troubles at your big event can be eased by knowing that you once ran a 10 k with a stomach full of chana masala and IPA.'

Transport for training

Bikes are brilliant. You can ride them to get to places. Fact. Commuting to work by bicycle won't just save you petrol money or bus fare, it will also sneak in some bonus miles and bike-handling practice in the time you might otherwise have spent being grumpy in a traffic jam. If you're close enough to the office, and lucky enough to have use of a shower when you get there, running is another great way of commuting. It's great exercise for your brain too, when you've worked out the logistics of planning where your towel and clean clothes will need to be. I've yet to master the swim commute, I must admit.

You don't have to limit your cycling or running to commuting. Laura once planned a cycle route from London to Peterborough to get in some miles and arrive in time for a beer festival, and I've cycled across two counties to get to my friend's hen weekend in the run-up to an ironman. Look on a map and see where half your race distance will take you. Put a few quid in your pocket and you could end up cycling to a new cafe, or on an adventure to somewhere you never knew existed; by the time you get home, you will have covered your triathlon course too.

Don't blow the budget

Maintaining the training-life balance means minimising stress, whatever the cause, so avoid financial strain by setting a budget and sticking to it. You may have noticed from your entry fee that triathlon can be expensive. That doesn't mean you need to get into debt preparing for your first race. Renting a wetsuit or borrowing a bike are both ways of mitigating some of the cost while you test the water in triathlon. No one wants to find themselves in the position of the man I once overheard at a race asking, 'How do I tell my pregnant girlfriend that I've just spend a thousand pounds on a wheel?'

Triathletes love kit and the sky is the limit when it comes to how much people can be prepared to spend. 'All the gear, no idea' is a phrase I've heard a lot in different sports; it's used to describe someone who has spent a lot on kit that they don't really know how to use. It was a taunt that concerned me when looking for my first road bike, worried that I'd get something too 'fancy' and not deserve it. My boyfriend's response to these misgivings was somewhat reassuring: 'Don't worry,' he said, 'there will always be someone with more gear and less of an idea.' It's a good thing to remind yourself of this when you turn up to races and gawp at the machines racked in the transition area.

Join the club

As Laura says, 'If you want to do something amazing, surround yourself with amazing people.'

A club, be it triathlon, running, swimming or cycling, is not just a source of training sessions, advice, and a bit of matching kit, it's also a great place to meet these people. Those who share your interests, outlook and goals, and those who can inspire you with stories about their own experiences, are those with whom you form some of the strongest friendships in life; making these friends through a sport may even see your training-life balance tip towards training becoming part of your social life, especially if you stay behind for a chat or a drink afterwards. It's much better than being the only one in the pub with goggle marks.

Imagine how great it would be to become one of these amazing people to someone else. Why not invite a friend or family member to join you on a swim, cycle or run and introduce them to what you're doing? If you have children, you can involve them too. I have some great memories of joining my mum for fun runs and bike rides, and cycling along with my dad when he went running; this time spent with them played a huge part in my interest in sport and I'm hugely grateful for a family that encouraged me to get outside. My brother's wife, Kathryn, an incredibly talented athlete who has raced at the World Ironman Championships in Hawaii, has two children who she inspires not only with her achievements but also by encouraging them to be active. At the very least, your family and friends get an insight into what you're working towards; even better, you get to spend some time together. What if they were inspired to give it all a go themselves? Just remember to rein in your competitive side: this isn't a race and there is no trophy for this win.

A matter of time

Everyone has stuff that's important – going to work, looking after kids, washing the untameable pile of training kit. But there also is a lot of space into which you can fit a swim, cycle or run if you really want to find it. It may mean getting up early in the morning for a swim, or parking the piece of work that could easily keep you at your desk, and leaving the office on time to get to a club session. Even have a look down the back of the sofa; we're probably all guilty of losing a few hours down there from time to time. Author and adventurer, Alastair Humphreys, talks about focusing on the '5–9' and working out what opportunities exist in those hours you're not at work: it's a good principle to apply to your training and even more crucial if, like many, you work longer or more awkward hours than the 9–5 template.

At the start of the week, plan when you're going to fit in your training and write it down. You could use a table like the one on the next page to block out the times when you have things you absolutely have to do – go to work, pick up kids, walk the dog etc; then colour in where your training sessions are going to be. Stick the table on your desk, fridge or wall as a visual reminder of the commitment you have made. Treating the key sessions like diary appointments that you cannot miss, and organising your kit so that you have no excuses when the time comes, can make it easier to stick to your plans; likewise, making sure that you factor in some time for rest and recovery or for a treat for all your hard work can help keep you motivated. Just think how pleased with yourself you'll be for the rest of the day if you do your swim first thing. If you're struggling to get out of bed, look your smug future self in the face and high-five them: you're off to the pool!

Mon	Tues	Weds	Thurs	Fri	Sat	Sun
6.00	6.00	6.00	6.00	6.00	6.00	6.00
7.00	7.00	7.00	7.00	7.00	7.00	7.00
8.00	8.00	8.00	8.00	8.00	8.00	8.00
9.00	9.00	9.00	9.00	9.00	9.00	9.00
10.00	10.00	10.00	10.00	10.00	10.00	10.00
11.00	11.00	11.00	11.00	11.00	11.00	11.00
12.00	12.00	12.00	12.00	12.00	12.00	12.00
13.00	13.00	13.00	13.00	13.00	13.00	13.00
14.00	14.00	14.00	14.00	14.00	14.00	14.00
15.00	15.00	15.00	15.00	15.00	15.00	15.00
16.00	16.00	16.00	16.00	16.00	16.00	16.00
17.00	17.00	17.00	17.00	17.00	17.00	17.00
18.00	18.00	18.00	18.00	18.00	18.00	18.00
19.00	19.00	19.00	19.00	19.00	19.00	19.00
20.00	20.00	20.00	20.00	20.00	20.00	20.00
21.00	21.00	21.00	21.00	21.00	21.00	21.00
22.00	22.00	22.00	22.00	22.00	22.00	22.00

Be nice

You've set yourself a challenge, you're working hard towards your goal, and we think you're a hero for this. Your loyal friends and family will also feel the same, especially if they see you doing something you love and you're feeling better for it. But remember that life goes on beyond your triathlon. The 'life' part of your training-life balance is important, changeable and sometimes unpredictable so also be prepared to compromise. Keep an eye on what you're like to be around and where your priorities are – if you're not prepared to move your run session for your mum's birthday lunch then you might need a little chat with yourself. Life happens, plans change, and it's not fair on your loved ones if your training becomes as strenuous for them as it is for you. And don't forget to thank them for their support.

R & R

Finally, there is some great news for you, and for your friends and family. The cherry on the top of the training-life balance pudding. Rest and recovery is really important. How much you need depends a bit on where you are starting and how much you are doing. I try to take one day a week off training completely; it tends to be on my busiest day at work, which probably doesn't count as proper rest, but it means one less thing to worry about when I'm really pushed for time. Remember how doing three sports is actually a really good thing? The order in which you plan your sessions can also help you get the most from your training by resting some muscle groups; for example, after a hard run, make your next session a swim, rather than cycling. Once a month, it's also sensible to have a lighter week where you reduce the intensity and duration of your sessions slightly. Looking after yourself by eating well, replacing fluid and getting enough sleep are vital too. A balanced training programme needs recovery periods built into it as it minimises the risk of overtraining and injury; even better, your body is processing all the training that you have done when you're recovering, so you'll be stronger as a result. So you can grab a cuppa, go back to that sofa for a bit, and relax – it all counts as training.

LAURA

Ironmania:
A weekend in Bolton

On the morning of Ironman UK in July 2014, I made myself a promise: I wouldn't end my race unless I absolutely had to and I would keep going until someone told me to stop. No matter how much I wanted it to be over, I would ask myself the question, 'Can I continue?' and if the answer was 'Yes', I'd carry on. My race would end prematurely after 7 hours and 60 miles. It almost ended a lot sooner, but I kept my promise.

I'd spent the previous two days living on a retail park in Bolton, which was the hub of the Ironman activity. It housed the registration tent, the bike to run transition, and a couple of thousand anxious triathletes. Everyone deals with their pre-race anxieties in different ways, while some want to talk about the race and all the training they have or haven't done in great detail with everyone and anyone who'll listen, my own way of trying to manage it was to pretend that the race wasn't happening. But with two days of pre-race faff – going to a race briefing, checking your bike in at T1, dropping your running kit at T2, familiarising yourself with the course while 2,000 other people do the same thing, some wearing Ironman T-shirts from other events and looking much more prepared than you – trying to ignore that it's actually happening proves very difficult.

By race morning, I was happy that all the race prep would finally be over and that I could just get on with the business of swimming, cycling and running. I was already awake when my alarm went off at 3.30 a.m. All that was left to do was to eat some breakfast, apply some number tattoos to my arms, and make my way to the start.

The sky had started to get light by the time I arrived at Pennington Flash Country Park. Despite the fact that 2,000 athletes were taking part, I bumped into a man who was staying at my hotel on the walk across a field to the bike rack. We passed a woman telling off her son. She was an anxious competitor and her son, presumably, was unenthusiastic about the early start. I sympathised with her son – I didn't want to be there either. I bumped into my cousin, Andy, too. This was his third iron-distance start line. He'd completed The Outlaw, in Nottingham, a couple of years earlier then, the year before, he'd started Challenge Henley but had been carted off in the back of an ambulance midway through. He was nervous that the same thing might happen again.

I found my bike, pulled off the yellow plastic cover that it had been underneath, keeping dry all night, and added my water bottles and fig rolls to its frame. I put my wetsuit on, dropped off the clothes I'd been wearing at the bag drop and, just like that, I was ready to start the race.

The start line was about 60 metres from the edge of the water so we began to swim out and then bobbed about waiting for the horn. The national anthem played and I turned to the guy next to me and said, 'I didn't know the Queen was taking part.' He laughed politely and I swam on to try to find a little more room for myself at the side of the pack.

I'd been anxious about the mass swim start: 2,000 other swimmers and me thrashing about in the water. But the start went better, much better, than I'd feared. I got punched and kicked a few times in the first 20 minutes and then again going round the buoys that marked out the course, but it was nothing too scary.

As we came around to the end of the first lap and Australian exit, where we would get out, run across a pontoon and get back in again, things started to go wrong. My goggles were pressing too tightly on my face and I felt a bit ropey. I was helped out of the water just as the elite men were finishing their second lap. I could see the timing clock: 46 minutes. I was right where I expected to be.

As I staggered along the carpet towards the re-entry point, I pulled my goggles off my face for some relief and so I could see where I was going. I sat down for a moment or two as I went to get back into the water. I felt sick but hoped a massive burp would sort it.

Back in the water, a hundred metres later, my goggles were filling up with water. I stopped, adjusted and continued. The same happened. Every hundred metres, I did the same again and the feeling in my stomach was getting worse. I stopped and held onto a kayak, thinking I was going to throw up. Another kayak joined us and I hung between the two. One of the kayakers gave me a bottle of orange squash to have a sip of. I thanked him and continued.

After rounding the last buoy to head back to the shore, the mass I'd been swimming in for the first lap had disappeared ahead of me. I was in a much smaller field of swimmers who were largely doing breaststroke. I knew I'd lost a lot of time. I tried to swim faster but my stomach was feeling worse and worse. Suddenly, I had to stop. There were no kayaks around to hold onto so I treaded water while I was sick. I wanted the race to end there and then, but I wasn't going to be dragged out of the water. If nothing else, I would finish the swim. I knew Katie and our friend, Liz, were out on the bike route waiting to cheer me on and I really wanted to see them.

I staggered out of the water again, down a tunnel of cheering spectators and found Phil. It had taken me 1 hour 54 minutes to do the 3.8 km swim; I was more disappointed in that than in what it meant for the rest of my day. A race official came over to check on me. He asked if I was OK and could I continue? I was worried he might withdraw me so I didn't mention being sick.

'I just need to get to my kit bag,' I said as I staggered off.

Inside the changing tent, I sat down shivering and drinking Cherry Coke. A woman came into the tent crying. 'It was going so well and then I got cramp,' she explained. She was crying because she was probably in the same situation as me: I knew I wasn't going to make the bike cut-off and that I wouldn't be allowed to finish the race. But I had made a promise to myself to keep going until that point, so after changing into my bike kit as quickly as I could, I staggered off again to find my bike.

The Ironman is a long race. Feeling rough at 7 a.m. in the morning makes the next 16 hours seem like an eternity. But it's also so long that it's possible to come out of the other side of a bad patch. To feel good again. I cycled past my hotel, briefly considering turning into the car park and climbing back into bed. But after less than an hour on the bike, I did start to feel OK.

A thick layer of mist obscured the highest point of the course as I turned a corner along Sheephouse Lane to make my ascent. It was one of the two hills that I'd been dreading for the past six months. As I slowly climbed up, I started overtaking other cyclists. The training I'd been doing with my coach, Chris, had paid off and I was feeling good on the hills. At the top, I saw Katie and Liz cheering. I whizzed past, ready for the downhills.

I knew from the moment that I climbed on my bike that I wouldn't make the bike cut-off. The cycle was going better than I'd hoped it would. I felt strong and was averaging a good pace, but I had lost more time on the swim than I could make up. If finishing a race in a certain time is your goal, it becomes difficult to keep going once you realise you're not going to make it. But I'd come here with a different goal. While I may have started out wanting to make it to the finishing line, that goal had evolved. I now wanted to enjoy my Ironman, however long it lasted. So as I made my way round the bike course, I looked at the countryside, tried to speak to other competitors, and smiled at the spectators. Every now and then, I'd look down at my average speed on my GPS, which told me I was making good progress and going faster than I'd hoped before starting, but I knew it wouldn't be enough to see me through to the finish.

After almost 60 miles on the bike, I rounded a corner, ready to climb up Sheephouse Lane again, but officials blocked off the road. I was the second rider to arrive just a minute after the intermediate cut-off had been put in place. More riders arrived behind me, some of them pleaded with the officials to continue, some of them got angry, and others got upset. I did none of these things. When I'd thought about being told I couldn't continue, in the weeks and months before the race, I imagined I would have got angry, or upset or have pleaded. But I was OK with it.

The officials took our timing chips off us and wrote down our numbers. 'There's a van coming to take you back.' I asked if I could cycle back instead. I didn't want to sit in a van with people that felt sorry for themselves or cheated out of being able to finish, and besides, the clouds had cleared and it was a nice day for a cycle.

'Are you sure you're OK to cycle?' the official asked.

'I'm more than fine. I've only done sixty miles.' I pedalled off, thinking about what I'd said. Only 60 miles? Six months ago, cycling 60 miles would have been a big deal. I might not have a finishers' medal, but that would only sit in a drawer. What I do have is legs that can cycle 60 miles without trouble.

I racked my bike, had a shower, was reunited with my supporters, and then headed to the finish. We drank beer, saw the first woman finish, drank more beer and then headed back out to cheer on the competitors who were finishing around the time I'd planned to complete the race. I wasn't sad that I wasn't one of them.

Before heading to Bolton, I'd booked a space in a pub in London for the following week and invited people to celebrate my post-Ironman life with me. I'd hesitated briefly: what if I didn't finish the race? I might have a mechanical problem with my bike, I could get too ill to continue, or I could simply not make the cut-off. How would the celebratory drinks go then? Should I wait until I'd done it and send the invite out then? Then I decided I didn't care.

I knew I could complete an iron-distance triathlon. I knew I was fit enough, strong enough and stubborn enough to swim 3.8 km, cycle 112 miles and run 26.2 miles. Whether I did it on one specific day in Bolton or not, I knew I could do an Ironman. I'd tested my body enough over the past 30 weeks and I'd got to know what it was capable of well enough to know that this, while not being easy, was something my body (and mind) could do. And I intended to celebrate that. Whether I was wearing my finisher medal or not, I intended to get drunk with some of the people who had supported me over the past few months and to celebrate being the fittest and strongest I'd ever been.

I'm glad I entered Ironman UK, even though I didn't finish it. My friend, Liz Goodchild, who was there to cheer me on says that goals should be big scary things that you're not entirely sure you can do. The Ironman fulfilled this role for me. That one day in Bolton had been the aim, but the journey to get there was so much more rewarding than I expected. I'd been out on long bike rides around parts of the countryside that I would never have seen if it wasn't for that race. I swam 3.6 km in a lido on a sunny Wednesday morning. I swam up and down for an hour and a half in the Serpentine. These are things that I wouldn't have tried, wouldn't have thought possible, and wouldn't have experienced if it wasn't for that big goal looming in the distance. And, although it wasn't the most pleasant swim of my life, I conquered my fear and swam 3.8 km with 2,000 people in Bolton.

I didn't know if I'd do another Ironman after Bolton, but I knew that I'd ride my bike for hours on end through the countryside, swim up and down in rivers, lakes and lidos and find new scary goals to chase down. I got a huge amount out of the Ironman that meant much more to me that the medal could ever have.

KATIE

The Bastion:
A long-haul triathlon

An aeroplane from Gatwick Airport rumbled across a blue sky and the sun began to fall behind me, casting a long shadow ahead on the trail. I looked up at the plane and wondered where it was off to, then down at the pair of unusually long legs created by a trick of the light; the shadow confirmed that they were now moving at a mere shuffle. It was 8.30 p.m. and I'd been running for nearly 5 hours.

•••

It was an aeroplane flying over my hotel that woke me up at 4.30 that morning, almost exactly a week before Laura's alarm went off in Bolton. Not that I'd slept particularly well before that. My alarm bleeped shortly after. I forced down some muesli and a cup of coffee, and made my way to the start of The Bastion, a new ironman event from the Castle Triathlon Series at Hever Castle in Kent.

Iron-distance triathlons are a bit like long-haul flights: they make me very nervous before they start; you see an awful lot of people wearing compression socks throughout; and you only get to consume food in really tiny portions. You also live in hope that you won't need to go for a poo at any point during the process; if you do, there is likely to be a long queue for a very cramped toilet.

This was my second ironman, the first being an event that ran through the night a year before; I was looking for a different challenge this time around and the possibility of taking part in daylight was a bonus. I had already encountered the hills of the half-iron version, The Gauntlet, with Laura at Hever the previous September, and there were many points where I was moving so slowly that I genuinely wondered how I was able to remain upright on my bike. It meant that no one was more surprised than me when I signed up for what had been billed as one of the most challenging courses in the UK.

Feeling so nervous before an iron-distance race took me a bit by surprise: I love race day normally and I'm always excited to get started. My nerves started to slip away as I lowered myself into the lake: I knew I had a long day ahead but there's nothing quite like swimming outside on a misty morning to calm me down. The 3.8 km swim took place beneath a drizzly sky in the early hours of Sunday morning, with the stunning surroundings of Hever Castle in the background; while posing no problem in the lake, the weather was causing a few anxious murmurs in the field about what this would mean for conditions on the bike course. My concerns lay less with what was falling from the sky and more with what lay ahead over the hills I'd be climbing.

Taking in a total ascent of more than 2,700 metres over the 180 km course, the organisers promised that the bike route would take in more climbing than any iron-distance event in the UK around at the time. Being at a bit of a disadvantage in the gravity department, I had questioned throughout my training whether I could finish the bike course within the time allowed. I promised to take it steady on the climbs, to keep fuelling up, and to keep smiling. With so many variables in a triathlon, it's easy to get caught up with worries about what might happen. I had to fix two punctures in the rain at my race the year before, and a heatwave had cut short my first attempt at the distance; staying positive is my way of remembering that you can only control the controllable things and there's no point worrying about something that hasn't actually happened, and might not. Within an hour or two, the clouds had cleared, drying the roads and finally making the descents an appealing change from the relentless peaks. Every so often, I'd be overtaken by someone who'd emerged behind me in the swim; many with a smile and a cheer, and one or two mumbling something about the hills in a way that made me wonder whether they'd actually read the website beforehand. With the sun high at midday, so too was the pollen count and the contents of my nose needed clearing all too frequently; I accepted that any weight loss must be helpful for climbing and continued to jettison snot rockets across the staggering countryside of Kent and East Sussex. It was only when I made it to the top of Ashdown Forest, the highest point in the race, for the sixth time, did I start to believe that the cut-off time was within reach.

There's a point in any flight when I look out of the window and think it's all a bit too amazing that we're still up in the sky. I know that the physics will explain how it's happening but I prefer not to question it and I just have to believe that we're going to stay up there. During the last hour of the cycle,

I'd started to think about whether I really 'needed' to do the run: perhaps it was a mix of exhaustion from the hills and elation that I had nearly completed the toughest part of the race; I'd completed marathons and an iron-distance race before so surely there was no harm in me stepping off my bike and quietly slipping off to the pub? I thought about Laura, about what she had achieved in the past two years, and about what she was preparing to do the following week at Ironman Bolton: she had told me her plan to keep racing unless someone told her to stop and I needed to make the same promise. As I rolled into transition, there could be no doubt in my mind that I would finish the marathon ahead; not because my legs felt particularly fresh (they didn't) or because marathon running is my strength (we all know it isn't) but because I'd already completed something that I wasn't really sure I could. Besides, if you let any doubts about finishing an ironman into your head, you're likely to descend into a nosedive from which it is very difficult to regain control.

I've found that the key is to think of the run not as a marathon. So I started by thinking of it as four laps instead. Four beautiful, hilly, muddy, technical, off-road laps. At 7 km I reached a feed station with such an array of goodies that I had to stop for a few minutes to consider carefully what I'd like. There, behind the plate of halved bananas and molten jelly babies, I spied an entire packet of those lovely Belgian caramel waffle biscuits and my eyes widened. These couldn't be for us? They are the kind of thing that I ask my boyfriend to put on a very high shelf at home for my own safety. 'Help yourself!' announced the marshal, presumably unaware of my superpowers when it comes to eating these things. I prised away a biscuit from the top of the packet and scampered away merrily in case there had been some kind of mistake. Moments later, it dawned on me that I would pass that aid station three more times. This was no longer a run of four laps, but an opportunity for four of those biscuits. I couldn't have been happier.

It was approaching 9 p.m. by the time I started my final lap; my hopes of finishing in daylight were dwindling so I grabbed my head torch and set off into the grounds of Hever Castle one last time. A winter of long runs and intervals with my running club must have done some good; I wasn't quick but I was still moving, and that was what mattered. With light fading rapidly and a full moon glowing behind the clouds, I reset my goal to make it home before the planes stopped flying over from Gatwick. I was slow and shattered and there were no in-flight movies for me, instead, I had to make my own entertainment: I sang as I ran alone through cornfields; I chatted to the lovely marshals, who were still smiling after being there for hours; and finally, as I ran down through the woods and another flight passed overhead, I stuck out my arms and made aeroplane noises to join in. Rabbits, caught in the beam of my head torch, looked on, unimpressed; perhaps they hadn't got my memo about staying positive.

From the darkness, I heard the commentator spot my light and cheer me onto the runway towards the finish. There were high-fives from my boyfriend and my parents as I banked in for landing, and I was allowed to run through the finishing tape, arms aloft, as if I'd won the thing; instead, it had taken over 16 hours, longer than any flight I've ever been on, and my only sight of the winners was when they each overtook me on their final lap of the run. A dedicated race organiser and his top notch crew were still there, after a very long day, ready with hearty congratulations; a medal was placed around my neck, while we chatted about the course and posed for photos with my supporters. The Bastion was no holiday but it was a first class event. Back in my hotel room, waiting to drop off to sleep, another aeroplane rumbled overhead. A little smile crept over my face: I'd completed the toughest race I'd ever tackled and I'd beaten the planes. I was also pleased I didn't live this close to an airport.

 **LAURA**

Striking while the iron is hot: 'The Iron Person'

My iron-distance triathlon didn't finish on a red carpet. There was no confetti, no medal, and no finisher's T-shirt. I just looked down at my watch as it silently ticked over to 26.2 miles. Then I stopped running and took a bow.

'That's it, she's done it.'

The small crowd, gathered outside the pub, exploded with cheers, whoops and laughter.

My iron-distance triathlon finished where the journey had begun on Christmas Eve seven months earlier, with me running along a path in Peterborough and with my dad riding alongside me on his bike. It wasn't the finishing line I'd expected, but it was perfect.

At 7.30 a.m. that morning, I stood by the side of Stoke Newington Reservoir: the only swimmer. It was a sunny morning and there was nobody on or in the water yet, just a few ducks swimming past. A safety kayaker walked up alongside me on the pontoon to get into his boat: 'You can get in, whenever you're ready.' He had no idea what I was about to attempt, very few people did. It was a plan that I'd hatched in the Lake District during the week's holiday I went on immediately after Bolton. I'd gone back and forth in my mind as to whether I wanted to try and do another iron-distance triathlon. I wanted some closure but I didn't want all the pre-event build-up that had made me so anxious last time.

'I imagine it's what tantric sex is like: my body has been building up to the distance for the past six months and now it needs some sort of release,' I'd explained to a friend.

I considered doing smaller races, to avoid the pomp and ceremony as much as possible, and then I realised I didn't have to do a race at all. I could wake up early on a Saturday morning, swim 3.8 km in the reservoir in London where I'd swum many times, then get on my bike and cycle 112 miles to Peterborough (the direct route is only about 90 miles so I'd throw in some diversions), and then, after a quick change of clothes at my sister's house, I would run 26.2 miles around the city. It would take a bit of planning to make sure everything and everyone I needed to make it happen was in the right place at the right time but, once you've successfully navigated the Ironman faff vortex, there's no pre-race prep too big to tackle. The more I thought about it, the more it appealed.

I got in the water without any fanfare, started my watch, and began swimming. The sun was still low in the sky and there was very little cloud, which made everything look very pretty but wasn't exactly ideal conditions for swimming in a straight line. I couldn't see the first buoy because the sun was straight behind it and, when I did turn around, the sun seemed to sit on my right shoulder and burn through my eyelids as I lifted my face to breathe. Some cloud would be nice, I thought.

I needed to swim five 750 metre laps plus the distance to and from the pontoon to make it up to the 3,800 m of a full iron-distance swim. A few other swimmers joined as I finished my first lap, but there was still plenty of space and I barely noticed them as they passed. At the far end of the reservoir, halfway round each lap, the water was choppier in the breeze. Small waves smacked me in the face and I bobbed about turning round the buoy. I'd thought a lot about what had made me sick during the Ironman UK swim and was now pretty certain it was 'sea sickness' made worse by nerves. I thought about taking sea sickness pills before this next attempt but I'd always been OK in the reservoir, and didn't feel nervous, so I forgot about it.

After my third lap, I stopped suddenly. I retched twice then three big mouthfuls of sick spilled out of me and floated in front of my face. I panicked – it was happening again. There was a safety kayaker behind me by the pontoon. I waved my hand through the water to disperse the evidence, worried that he'd ask me to leave the reservoir. Then I put my face back in the water and swam off. I felt awful during the next lap. My stomach ached and the sensory deprivation of swimming, not seeing or hearing very much, made it difficult to focus on anything other than the churning in my gut. I swam tentatively towards the far end of the reservoir, knowing that the rocking motion of the waves wouldn't help. As I swam back to the pontoon for the end of lap number four, I had resigned myself to ending the swim at 3,000 metres. Three km was still a long way, and this was my event so I could make the rules. I climbed out of the water, took my goggles off and sat down.

There were three cut-off times to my event. These weren't arbitrary numbers that I'd set upon. They had real meaning and consequences. Firstly, I hoped the whole thing would be over in time for me to make it to the pub for last orders; I also wanted to get off the bike before my nieces went to bed at 7 p.m. For the swim leg, the cut-off time hadn't been decided by me: instead, the swim session at Stoke Newington Reservoir ran from 7.30 until 9.30 a.m. I had time to do one last lap. After a minute or two of sitting on the deck, I put my goggles back on and headed back into the water. I headed to the first buoy and was feeling fine, I headed to the second buoy and was swimming faster. The faster I swam, the stronger I felt. As I pulled myself out of the water once more, I was excited that I'd done it, but more importantly, that I'd got back in and finished the job.

My transition from swim to bike was a very relaxed affair and would set the tone for the rest of the day. I saw my friend, Josie, in the changing rooms. 'Go, go, go!' she shouted as I left to the bewilderment of everyone else getting changed. I had time to find a lost purse in the toilets and hand it in to reception before heading outside to my bike, which Phil had wheeled around from his flat.

'I was sick three times, but I did it.'

'Oh no. Why do you keep being sick?'

'I don't know and I don't care – it doesn't matter anymore after today because I'll have done it. I don't have to do it again.'

He took my wetsuit and I pedalled off to do laps of Finsbury Park to clock up some miles while I waited for him to join me for the long cycle north. I was on my fifth lap of the park when I saw him again and was getting pretty fed up of going up and down the same two hills. He gave me a can of Coke to settle my stomach and, after a few glugs, I did a burp so loud it felt as though the ground shook. A woman talking on the phone more than 60 metres away gave me a look of absolute disgust. I like to think that Phil was a little proud of me.

We headed through a few miles of North London Saturday morning traffic, sitting behind buses and waiting at traffic lights, before the roads calmed down a bit. We'd done the route before as a training ride for Bolton, stopping overnight at my friend, Helen's house, two thirds of the way up in St Neots, so we knew where we were going. Our route traced the train line back to Peterborough where I'm from and it took us through places that I'd only previously known as stations where people got off and on: Hitchin, Arlesey, Biggleswade, Sandy. It was still sunny and breezy, and rolling along country roads was a way I'd have probably chosen to spend the day, whether I was doing this ridiculous challenge or not. That had been one of the things that amused me before Bolton: how silly it all was. It was essentially a bit of swimming, cycling and running to an arbitrary length. Somehow, put together and given an intimidating name, it became so much more than that. I'd heard people use the rhetoric of going to war to describe their triathlons. How I felt as I rolled along through Cambridgeshire, getting ever closer to my nieces' bedtime, was very different to that. I felt free.

I texted my brother at around 50 miles in. Somewhere between St Neots and Huntingdon, a car headed towards us beeping; my brother was leaning out of the window waving at us. We pulled over for a chat and a snack and he filled up our water bottles. We saw him a couple more times as he drove ahead then stopped to take photos of us. A few miles after passing Huntingdon, we headed out onto the Fens. The Fens are an area of East Anglia that used to be under water.

Now, thanks to a lot of dykes, they're very much land, very flat land and with some very straight flat roads intersecting them. What the Fens lack in hills, they make up for in wind. It's a rule of triathlon that you aren't allowed to draft the rider in front of you; in a long-distance event, you have to keep at least 10 metres between you and their rear wheel unless you're overtaking, which must be done within a set time or you must drop back. As we headed into a headwind after several hours of riding it was tempting to have Phil pull in front of me so I could shelter from the wind, but the no drafting rule was one of the few official rules I had planned to adhere to (along with not dropping litter) and, as such, he spent most of the day riding behind me. The benefit of the flatness of the Fens though is that you can see Peterborough on the horizon as you approach from quite some distance. I let out an excited yelp when I first caught a glimpse of the spiky outline of Peterborough Cathedral still about 15 miles away. Each time I looked up from the road in front of me, it was getting closer and closer until we were passing the end of my sister's road. I'd cycled 100 miles and couldn't yet stop. The next 6 miles were hard. We headed straight out of the city towards Oundle, again into a headwind. And then it started to rain. At 106 miles, we could turn round with the wind on our backs and know that, in less than half an hour, we'd be off our bikes.

My nieces were still up when I staggered into their garden. 'I've never been so pleased to get off my bike,' were the first words out of my mouth. Not because I hadn't enjoyed the cycle, because I had, but because climbing off my bike meant that I'd done it: I'd finished the bike leg and there was just the small matter of a marathon to run.

My running kit, that had been brought up from London the week before by my parents, was laid out ready for me. I drank some more Coke and ate some crisps.

'Transition is a lot less dynamic than I expected it to be,' said my brother-in-law, Rob. He was converting his bike into a mobile feed station ready to cycle alongside me as I ran 26.2 miles. He loaded up the panniers with drinks, crisps, energy gels and toilet roll. There was no situation we weren't prepared for.

'It's nearly seven o'clock. Do you think I can run a marathon in less than five hours?'

'Yes, but you've got to hurry up and get your act together,' came the reply.

My two nieces, Molly and Darcey, my sister, Emma, and Phil all waved us off as we headed off down the street. For the first half, we stuck pretty close to the route of the Great Eastern Run half marathon that I'd done five times and yet kept forgetting where exactly it went. Every few miles, Rob would cycle ahead of me and open up his panniers so that I could grab a gel or a drink. As we headed back towards the town centre, around 10 miles into the run, my brother's car pulled up again, this time he had company. He unloaded a bike and my dad got on it and joined my mobile support crew. It was starting to get dark and my two cyclists turned on their lights.

My favourite parts of the run all happened in those last couple of hours after it got dark. We headed through the city centre; it was Saturday night and the bars were full of people. Some stood outside waiting to get in or having a cigarette. As I ran past, some looked at me, possibly thinking it was a little late for a jog, others shouted out at me. All of them had no idea what I was doing, how far I'd cycled, swam or run that day. I didn't need them to know because I knew. We headed back over the town bridge and towards the almost halfway point at the Palmerston Arms pub, my parents' local. My mum was outside waiting with Phil. I nipped inside to use the toilet and get some water.

'Just run a marathon have you?' a man at the bar joked. I looked down at my GPS watch. 'No, I'm halfway through actually.' He looked at me, not sure if I was joking.

The three of us, Dad, Rob and I, set off again this time towards Ferry Meadows, a country park made up of three big lakes. As we turned off the main road towards the park I turned my headtorch on. I ran along the path through the trees in darkness with three circles of light showing me where to put my feet. As we rounded the far side of the biggest lake, I could hear the waves gently breaking against stones a couple of metres to my left and music quietly drifting over the water from a party at the watersports centre on the other side. A bright moon was out and lit up the lake and we went past some shadowy figures out fishing where they shouldn't have been. There were more people out in the darkness than I'd expected: the fishermen, the occasional dog walker, a couple of teenagers chatting, and an elderly couple on their way home from the party we could hear.

At around 22 miles, I thought I might be sick, or worse. But the feeling passed as soon as it came. At no point during the day had I willed it to be over but now I was increasingly ready to finish. As we exited the park and headed towards the main road, my path split from the one being used by my support riders for a couple of hundred metres and we were separated by some large bushes.

'Sing so we know you're OK!' they instructed.

Plod, plod, plod: my feet landed in time to my rendition of Daft Punk's 'Get Lucky', the lyrics feeling ever more appropriate as I ran through the dark.

The last couple of miles were hard. I'd taken my dad out running that winter and distracted him from wanting to stop with games I play with my beginner runners – taking turns to name countries, cities, pop groups, anything in alphabetical order.

'OK, I'll start,' he said as we approached the last mile. 'Australia.' We went three times through the alphabet.

I ran down a side road and back, and around a car park twice in that last mile. I could see the pub ahead but my mileage wasn't close enough to allow me to head straight for it. As I approached the pub, I could see my mum, Phil and a group of regulars stood outside. I turned down the road opposite the pub watching my GPS click through fractions of a mile. I turned around to face the pub, ran another hundred metres towards it and then I was done.

Sixteen hours and 15 minutes after I'd got into the water by myself, I stopped running surrounded by people who had supported me, not just that day but for the past couple of years. It was probably the most fun day I've ever had, and although I was the only competitor in my iron-distance triathlon, I wasn't alone. It was perfect.

Epilogue

I've just had a potentially stupid/amazing idea to do a 3.8 km swim, a 112 mile cycle and a 26.2 mile run wherever and whenever I want to.

This sounds brilliant. You could call your event the iron(ic)man. The irony being that you're not a man.

The iron(ic)man will be going ahead in two weeks! Swim in London, cycle to Peterborough, then run the marathon escorted by my dad on his bike.

Katie

Over the past two years, Laura and I have had a lot of conversations: some about triathlon; some about running; some about books, or blogs, or beer festivals. Many of them have happened by email or by text message. The majority of them have made me laugh out loud, and, as I read back through them, they still do. This one, from the week after Bolton, just left me in awe.

Sadly, I already had a holiday planned and I wouldn't be around for Laura's homemade iron-distance triathlon. If I had been in the country, I would have cheered, and marshalled, and ridden on a bike alongside her. Not because I was in any way worried about her, or her ability to complete it. I just wanted to be involved with what sounded like a perfect day.

We were more worried about Laura when we heard that she hadn't made the cut-off in Bolton. With so much invested in the months leading up to it, we worried that she'd be upset, disappointed, or cross. But she was none of those things. Instead, she found a pub with good beers and karaoke, within walking distance of the run course, and insisted that we all went back to cheer on the remaining competitors on the course. We learned then that there was no need to worry about Laura.

After Bolton, Laura wanted to find a fun way to cover the iron-distance: something cheaper than the traditional way of entering a race; something that would capitalise on her fitness and preparation, without waiting months for the right event to appear; something that would encourage other people, who might be put off by the expense, or the mass swim starts, or any negative things they might have heard about triathlons, to have a go and to do their own DIY triathlon of any distance.

Laura filmed her triathlon and put it onto her blog after the event. There was a 'Snickers energy gel' (when the weather got the better of her snack), crisps in T2, and the 'Eye of the Tiger' playing from a mobile phone as she ran. There were laughs and smiles, and the people closest to her were all enjoying the day.

The 'iron(ic)man' moniker didn't last long and it was soon renamed by Laura: the 'Iron Person' was suggested in the run up to Ironman UK, by one of Laura's colleagues who couldn't understand why such an iconic event would give itself a name that only seemed to include half of the population. Women only make up about a quarter of participants in triathlon events at the moment and it isn't really enough. We'd both like to see this change and Laura's triathlon was just one small shift in the right direction, even if it wasn't a race. The name stuck.

For most of us, participating in triathlon will involve taking part in an event: a race. I love racing and I'll keep entering events as long as I am enjoying the sport. For me, triathlon is a hobby: it's something I choose to do; it's something I pay to do. Enjoyment is key. There are always cheaper ways to have a rubbish time on a Sunday morning. We tend to see triathlon as something that is comprised of three sports that only happen together on race day and in a competitive environment, but it doesn't have to be. Laura and I both welcome anyone to call themselves a triathlete: to enter a race, big or small, long or short, and throw themselves fully into the world of triathlon. Or to do what Laura did and enjoy a big day out doing three sports. Just remember: there are no such things as bad races, just good stories.

Laura

The condition known as 'post-race blues' is common among athletes of all levels. It's easy to understand why: you spend a good proportion of your year focused on one goal; your days and weeks are structured around it; you look forward to it and, in a weird way, you also hope it never arrives. Then, once it's over and the initial euphoria or disappointment has gone, and your legs have stopped complaining, you're left with quite a bit more spare time on your hands and nothing on the horizon to inspire you.

Over the past six months, I'd become a master of utilising my time: running to work; waking up early for a swim before the sun is even up; and doing one-legged squats while brushing my teeth. I'd combined seeing friends with doing runs, having a beer after a track session, or training together on the weekend. Pretty much every hour of my week was filled with something. After putting a big tick through 'Do an iron-distance triathlon', I was fully prepared to sink into a bad mood for a few weeks. But it didn't happen.

For weeks, I'd joked that I was looking forward to ironman training being over so that I would no longer have a massive pile of washing-up sitting in the kitchen for most of the week. The event came and went, my legs recovered quickly and still the piles of washing-up sat in the kitchen. I went to visit friends, I got drunk, I danced like a lunatic and I crawled into bed at 4 a.m. If I hadn't been having so much fun, I might have realised that this was the same time a few weeks earlier that I was up and preparing to start my swim in Bolton. I'd looked forward to sitting on the sofa of an evening, watching rubbish TV, and not having any training to do. But when the choice between doing the washing-up, sitting on the sofa, and going for a run, swim or cycle presented itself, I still chose one of the latter because they were the parts of my week that I enjoyed the most. My weeks still looked similar to how they had during training. Most days still included a swim, cycle or run of some sort – albeit at a slower pace or for fewer miles.

Once you've accounted for going to work and sleep, there aren't that many hours left in your week. Triathlon training had made me value those precious hours and it changed how I chose to spend them. I have now found time to do the washing-up and you'll still find me watching rubbish TV, but these aren't pressing matters and neither will get in the way of me saying 'Yes!' to most invites to go for a swim or a bike ride.

I said yes to an invite to take part in an Ironman 70.3 relay in Zell, Austria, just a few weeks after my own iron-distance triathlon. I took on the run leg with two people I'd never met before who were doing the swim and cycle. Neither of my teammates had done a triathlon before and, as we navigated the pre-race faff of putting our bags in various locations, checking in the bike, and going to the race briefing, I found myself answering their questions and quelling their fears. Supported and encouraged along the way by Katie, I'd learnt a lot about triathlon in the past couple of years and now I was passing it on. The greatest lesson I'd learnt was that it doesn't matter about your finish position, the true test of a successful race is how much you enjoy it, and we all enjoyed our race that day. I might always be one of the last competitors crossing the finishing line of a triathlon, but in terms of enjoyment I'm hoping to podium every time.

Acknowledgements

Laura

When I tell people about my Iron Person, one of the dominant reactions I get is 'Wow, what an amazing support network you've got'. And I agree; I'm very lucky to have people around me who support me and want to help me achieve my goals. It's not just on that one day in August, but every day.

My mum and dad, the 'Mustard Pots', so called because of their distinctive yellow jackets that help me spot them in the crowd at races, have been a permanent fixture at my marathons and triathlons, always ready with a bottle of beer at the finish line. I'd like to thank them, Big Phil, my brothers and sister, Mark, Karl and Emma for their support.

I met my boyfriend, Phil, nine years ago. I didn't run then and couldn't swim, and I'm pretty sure he never imagined that a few years later he'd spend a good proportion of his weekends roped into some sort of running, cycling or swimming adventure. Thankfully it's something that he's embraced and encouraged me to do more of. Thanks Phil.

My friend Helen has put me up the night before races, woken up at a ridiculous hour to drive me to the start and shown more genuine interest in the silly things I do than you could imagine. So I want to thank her too. Liz Goodchild, thanks go out to you for the straight talking and keeping me sane when I've wanted to cry and quit.

Thanks too to triathlon coach Chris Langley-Weylan for some great advice in the run-up to Bolton. I was more prepared than I would have been without it and I've pretty much forgiven you for making me go up Swains Lane five times in a row.

The Serpentine Running Club set me up with Stephanie, the best, most bonkers swim coach I could have hoped for, Tuesday track sessions and support in becoming a running coach myself. Thanks guys, you're a brilliant club.

My colleagues have come to accept that the pile of soggy kit by my desk from me cycling and running to work is a permanent fixture of our office now. They allowed me to change my working hours to better accommodate all the training in the run-up to the Ironman and haven't yet told me to shut up about it. Thank you all.

Will Wriggly, my sports massage therapist of many years, has seen me hobble into his office distraught that my latest injury is going to ruin all my plans, and has patched me up and helped me get to the start line of all the races I've planned to do. Thanks Will.

Finally, thank you Katie. You've made me laugh with pretty much every email and message for the past few years and, more recently, with every chapter you sent over. You have made the impossible enjoyable.

Katie

One cold afternoon at work in January 2012, I received a message from Laura on Twitter:

> Thinking of doing a tri so I was going to ask you for tips. Then I wondered if you would write guest blog post for me?

Triathlon has been lurking around in my family since the days when people used to compete in their swimming trunks (there are photo albums at my parents' house with pictures to prove this). Steve and Rob – the kind of brothers a little sister is proud to have – were the first people I knew who did triathlon, not to mention all sorts of other adventures that I've wanted in on ever since. My parents, Pete and Miriam, are, of course, to thank for all of this; for nurturing the kind of family where being active is totally normal and setting the best possible example in this respect. They've driven miles to watch me in anything from a 25-metre race in a swimming gala to an iron-distance triathlon that took significantly longer than I think they were bargaining on. Thank you, Mum and Dad.

My brothers taught me everything I know about breaking bikes; everything I know about mending them comes from my very patient boyfriend, Danny. He has fixed my bike, driven across France, waited on a roundabout in the rain, and slept in the back of his car to support me at races. Thanks for your patience when I was writing chapters on our only mutual day off work each week, and for reminding me that things often become clearer after a bike ride and a nice cup of coffee.

Emily W., Gordon and Charlie are my 'urban family' and they go to prove that friends made through sport (and a mutual love of good dinners) are some of the finest ones you'll ever know. Thank you for the fun times rowing, then swimming, cycling, or running since.

I've enjoyed cycling with lots of people since I got my first road bike: among them, Mary, who wisely refused to share Vaseline between John O' Groats and Land's End; Rachel and Helen, from OUCC, who answered all my questions when I wanted to do a triathlon; Zappi's ladies and Chris, who let me make up the numbers at the 9-up from time to time and introduced me to Anita and Emily L., who have accompanied me on many training rides, nattered over coffee, or checked chapters from this book. Thank you to my triathlon club, Oxford Tri, and my workplace, who had the good sense to put on swimming sessions in the pool 20 metres from my office, and who finally got me back into the water and enjoying swimming again after nearly 15 years.

I took Laura up on her offer and wrote that guest post; I've never regretted it. Laura is one of those people you'll meet in life who is always full of ideas but what really sets her apart is how she follows up on them and turns them into reality. This book is just one of those ideas. Thanks to our editor, Sophie Martin, at Summersdale, for all your help with the manuscript, and for laughing in all the right places. And, finally, thank you, Laura, for having the faith in me to join you in this idea.

If you're interested in finding out more
about our books, find us on Facebook at
Summersdale Publishers and follow
us on Twitter at **@Summersdale**.

www.summersdale.com